Christina -

Thanks so much
for all the
support in making
things happen!
Really enjoyed it
+ excited about
your new adventures.

Sharah

05/03/24

For Aida – for supporting me through my own inflection moments

Praise for Inflection

"A book of equivalent weight and importance to Oliver Burkeman's Four Thousand Weeks. A powerful call for how we can each step forward and address our most pressing leadership challenges today".

> Amy Major, MBA Programme Director, Said Business School, University of Oxford

"Timely, inspiring, and thought-provoking, Inflection offers a new model for leaders seeking authenticity and excellence in an ever-changing world."

> Alice Sherwood, author of *Authenticity: Reclaiming Reality in a Counterfeit Culture*

"Inflection is a superb example of how, as leaders, we can utilise a strategic lens to consider the ebb and flow of leadership and performance. Inflection shows the gains that can be made by understanding when, how and if change can be embedded, slowed, accelerated and in some cases stopped. This is an excellent companion to any senior leader who wants to be working on their organisation, as well as within it."

> Dan Morrow, CEO, Dartmoor Multi Academy Trust

"Inflection is about helping us as leaders zoom out, to help us understand our role in an organisation and how we nurture those around us. In our ever-complex world, that balance is hard. Identifying role models that are doing it well, can be even harder. This book equips you with a moment to reflect for yourself and ask powerful questions, to help you think about a next step forward."

> Salma De Graaff, Chief Human Resources Officer, Skyscanner

"Inflection creates frameworks that guide your thinking and at the same time leaves space for agility in how they are implemented. The complement of simple tools like the watch analogy, make these easy to build into our mental models. The focus on how leaders develop, what to keep and what to leave behind, is immensely liberating. It's the key to real growth and development."

> Cynthia Hansen, Managing Director, Innovation Foundation (empowered by Adecco Group)

"Having recently gone through our very own inflection moment at JKS, so much of Inflection really resonated. The book helps us all as Leaders change how we see and understand Inflection Moments, as well as build powerful new principles into our day- to-day practice."

Sunaina Sethi, People Director, JKS Restaurant Group

"Compassion, insight and vision combined with practical advice. This is an invaluable addition for any leadership bookshelf."

Julia Hobsbawm, commentator, Bloomberg Work Shift and author of *The Nowhere Office & Working Assumptions*

"As we all seek to navigate rapid change, the challenges of leadership have never been greater. This is the right book at the right time."

Lord Jim Knight, Member of the House of Lords and Former National Education Minister

INFLECTION

A ROADMAP FOR LEADERS
AT A CROSSROADS

SHARATH JEEVAN OBE

Table of Contents

Section 3: The Minute Hand: Ignite Potential in Ourselves and Others   **39**

SECTION 1:

RECOGNISING OUR LEADERSHIP INFLECTION MOMENTS

---

*I*n this first section, we'll start by defining what inflection moments really are – and why they are so critically important for ourselves, our organisations and societies at large. We'll look at the limitations of existing leadership thinking – particularly the assumption that all leadership time is created equal. We'll also look at the internal and external triggers of an inflection moment and how, as leaders, we can proactively recognise and respond to them. Finally, we'll introduce the DIAL framework and the timeframes we need to consider at inflection moments – the hour hand (long-term), the minute hand (medium-term), the second hand (short-term) and the overall learning dial.

In this part of the book, we'll cover the following micro-chapters:

- A Crisis in Leadership: From Disillusionment to Hope

- Throwing Out the Playbook: Outdated Mental Models of Leadership

- The Tyranny of Time: Our Nemesis as Leaders

- Asteroids and Starships: The Threat and Opportunity of Inflection Moments

- High Stakes, Big Prizes: A Chance to Futureproof Your Success

1: A Crisis in Leadership: From Disillusionment to Hope

You're not sure which has changed more – you or the world around you.

Irrespective, the dials on your leadership watch have stopped ticking. To be honest, they've been slowing down for a while.

You might have spent years – even decades – setting your life to other people's watches. All because you thought they actually knew what they were doing.

You thought they were the proverbial grown-ups. You thought they had the answers. Now you know they were simply wearing the emperor's new clothes.

If you're an established leader, you may have all the trappings of success: the fancy title, a comfortable pay packet and a glamorous office with – finally – some well-earned flexibility. But these perks just aren't as satisfying as they used to be. You're not ungrateful, but you want more.

If you're an emerging leader, you may feel deeply uneasy about what you're hurtling towards. You see a paradox: a world needing leadership more than ever, while many leaders don't even seek out real problems to solve and instead become increasingly obsessed with serving themselves.

You want to set your own leadership dials now in order to be truly authentic. And you want to see the dials move at the same pace, whether you are at work or at home. You want to be helping those immediately around you – your colleagues, family and friends – but also, more broadly, you want to be shaping a better world. Most of all, you want to break this cycle of emptiness and cynicism you've seen so many of your peers and role models fall prey to.

You're not sure whether much of what you've been taught about leadership really fits any more. The idea of the leader providing the right answers seems redundant; there seem to be so few 'right' answers nowadays, and certainly no golden rules that stand up to scrutiny. You can't seem to just tell people what to do or to think anymore – whether it's your colleagues or even your own child. They want a lot more from you, and in all honesty, you're not sure you can provide it. Often, it feels like you need them more than they need you.

Meanwhile, the world around you grows ever more volatile – hurtling from a pandemic to the cost-of- living crisis in a heartbeat.

The majority of the hundreds of leaders I work with are wracked by internal and external turbulence and unsure how to navigate where they and their organisations should go next.

Is it still even possible to lead in times like these? There's good news: the answer is yes.

The more difficult news is that to do so, you'll need to throw out a lot of your preconceived notions and mental models of leadership. In the next micro-chapter, we'll explore exactly why these mental models are so out of date for the extraordinary times we are living in.

But there is still opportunity and cause for optimism in leadership. I hope you'll embark on this journey with me, over the coming micro-chapters, towards creating much more hopeful times – for ourselves, for the people we lead and care about and for us all.

2: Throwing Out the Playbook: Outdated Mental Models of Leadership

Why are our mental models of leadership past their sell-by date?

Last year, I spent a bitterly cold November morning with Janet Dugdale and Rebecca Loy on the Liverpool docks. These two brave museum leaders are helping this great city reconcile with its past because Liverpool was an epicentre of the global slave trade.

They are doing this openly and sensitively, inviting historians, residents and community groups to come together and reflect on the city's history so that they can build a collective narrative. They don't know what that narrative will be and how it might help to shape the city's future, but they are still willing to lead this challenging and uncertain journey. They don't have outcomes set in stone, they aren't dictating the process and they're not focused on 'making the problem go away'.

Leadership like this – bravely voyaging into the unknown – isn't quite going the way of the dodo, but why is it increasingly becoming an endangered species?

I think it's because we've succumbed to three leadership obsessions, none of which has proven healthy.

The first obsession has been about finding the perfect response to every specific situation. There's the overused observation about Churchill being a great war leader but a hopeless peacetime one. Perhaps to offset this risk, great companies where I used to work (eBay, for example) had 'playbooks' to help leaders know exactly what to do in different situations.

But our playbooks cannot predict and solve every possible situation. How useful have playbooks been in coping with extreme and unpredictable events such as the COVID-19 crisis or the current cost-of-living crisis? On the other hand, I have seen and supported leaders who have been able to flourish in very different situations by adapting their skills. The difference is they have known how to navigate a specific context rather than following a set of predetermined 'rules'.

The second (especially recent) obsession has been about authenticity. We all want to remove the 'mask' of inauthenticity: to be the same person leading others as we are as a friend, parent or spouse.

There's a lot to be said for authenticity. Yet I have seen many leaders with high potential go up in flames on its pyre. If we're not careful, it can lead to us indulging our own whims and therefore not focusing fully on the people we are trying to help and serve. We'll redefine authenticity with a much more helpful – and specific – explanation later on, in the third section of the book.

The third (and perhaps oldest) obsession has been around trying to identify the critical traits of great leaders. What do we need to be in order to succeed? This might be charismatic, decisive or whatever the latest leadership fad is.

Among the hundreds of established and emerging leaders I've worked with, there is nothing like a catalogue of stable traits that I can point to that defines success. Indeed, all too often, leaders are written off – unfairly and prematurely – because they are not perceived to have these 'right' traits.

We'll delve into a different framing of leadership in subsequent micro-chapters, but understanding the limitations of this situations – authenticity – traits (SAT) triangle is a powerful starting point.

As we'll explore, we need more leaders like Janet and Rebecca who are willing to voyage into the unknown.

Isn't it time we took these unhelpful mental models of leadership off our proverbial shelves?

3: The Tyranny of Time: Our Nemesis as Leaders

What's our biggest struggle as leaders?

It's not what we often think: the struggle for money, power and resources. It's the struggle against time.

No matter how much wealth or power we accumulate, most of us will have about 4,000 weeks to live. And 90,000 hours to make a difference in our working lives. There's a powerful finality in these two numbers.

I love author Oliver Burkeman's perspective that we have embraced productivity to its hilt. And that we now need to accept the limitations of time – that we can't do everything.

But as leaders there are two particular dynamics that make this truth so much more challenging today.

The first dynamic is that we need to juggle the demands of the hour hand (our long-term direction), the minute hand (our medium-term potential) and the second hand (our day-to-day motivation and resilience). That's always been the case of course, but today the second and minute hands move at the speed of light. As we know, what feels urgent often trumps what is truly important; it's so easy, therefore, for the hour hand (our long-term direction) to be neglected. We need a learning dial that helps us to continually refine and correct this balance given the limited time we ultimately have to reach these end goals. (We'll dive much deeper into these hands and the dial throughout this book).

The second dynamic is the critical importance of inflection moments. These tend to be make-or-break moments in our leadership and our lives when something deeply changes in ourselves, our organisation or in the external environment around us. In these times, we have a chance to futureproof success for ourselves, our organisations and the people we serve – or to lay the foundations for failure. Not all time is created equal, and these moments provide a special opportunity to transform our future. As the urgency of our lives has sped up, inflection moments take on an ever more outsized importance. They provide one of the few opportunities we have as leaders to really imagine the mountain we next want – and need – to climb.

There are three types of leadership inflection moments. The first are personal – they relate to our own career and lives. These could be navigating a career change or a mid-career shift, to take just two examples. The second are organisational – a new chapter in our organisation's life or narrative, driven by an internal or external change. The third are societal – for instance, how we, as leaders, can craft new approaches to inequality or climate change.

The focus of this book is squarely on the first two types of inflection moments – the personal and the organisational – and on how the two often intertwine. Though, of course, they have knock-on implications for how leaders can contribute in the most powerful way to these big societal inflection moments.

In the first micro-chapter, I described a leader going through the first of these – their own inflection moment; a personal or leadership transition perhaps driven by dissatisfaction and disillusionment or something more positive like a new outlook on what really matters. As London Business School professor Lynda Gratton points out, these transitions can happen at any time of our lives, and they aren't always synchronised with our peer groups. Because of this, they can feel deeply lonely. If they occur at the same time as organisational or industry-wide inflection moments, this only complicates things. We may feel confused as to what to do next and therefore rudderless despite the urgency of our ever- dwindling time.

That feeling is all too common among the leaders I work with.

As we'll delve into later on, we have to learn to navigate the hour, minute and second hands on our own terms.

Here's the paradox: as leaders, we can never fully conquer time. But equally, we mustn't let it conquer us.

4: Asteroids and Starships: The Threat and Opportunity of Inflection Moments

Inflection moments make or break leaders.

And they define the future of organisations and sectors for years – sometimes decades – to come. But how do you know when you are about to face one?

I think there are two telling signs to look out for.

The first – look out for the asteroid. Something fiery in the stratosphere that you are about to collide into, head-on.

It's usually a significant shift in the external environment around you.

A change in the market or sector that you operate in, or in a government policy that affects you. It could also be a change in public opinion on an issue, or how your organisation is perceived or governed.

Asteroids often emerge out of sight. While we may be aware of a threat hovering in the distance, we can't do much as leaders to temper their fire or speed.

The second – look within your own starship. Think of the Starship Enterprise or Battlestar Galactica. They're our own teams, units, organisations or families. Places where we have much more control.

You've got your own crew on the starship, and you probably feel much more comfortable within its sanctum. Yet, even the most capable leaders – think of Jean-Luc Picard or even Spock – find themselves wracked with self-doubt on the Enterprise. (If they didn't, we would have half as many Star Trek episodes as we do now). And that's where paralysis can seep in.

Perhaps you're feeling a sense of drift. The sense that you or your team are not realising your potential. Or the sense that your team may be 'quietly quitting' in front of your very eyes.

Be especially wary of the complacent starship. Remember Picard's refrain to 'boldly go where no man has gone before'. We want to feel like we are alive and growing – cruising our galaxy intentionally and at speed.

What makes leading through inflection moments so difficult is that we can't afford to keep our starship at a standstill, but neither can we risk crashing into the asteroid.

The most successful leaders I have worked with do something rather ingenious instead.

They harness the threat of the asteroid to keep their starships evolving in a new direction.

A direction they believe is truly right and which taps into their own motivations and convictions. (An area we'll delve into in subsequent micro-chapters).

I'm not a huge sci-fi fan myself, but here's what I've learned about leadership: it's the combined threat and opportunity of starships and asteroids that makes inflection moments so challenging to navigate as leaders.

But it's exactly this tension of opportunity and challenge that I would argue is the essence of leading today.

It's what makes leading so deeply relevant and important in these turbulent times. It's what keeps us deeply alive as leaders in the first place.

5: High Stakes, Big Prizes: A Chance to Futureproof Your Success

Why are inflection moments so hard to navigate? And why are they 'make or break' for leaders? Usually, there are several dynamics at play that create this complexity.

First, you have to be able to recognise the stop sign and the fork in the road. Many leaders don't, particularly when they feel like they're already successful and on cruise control. Acknowledging that the future will be different to the present takes courage and humility.

Second, they often come in twos – an external shift and an organisational shift. This is the asteroid I mentioned in the previous micro-chapter – a sector-wide or even a global shift (I just heard Sundar Pichai, managing director of Google, describe AI as one of our most profound global inflection moments) accompanied by an internal change within the starship (in leadership, governance or strategy within an organisation). Trying to avoid the asteroid while navigating the changes within your starship is a tough balancing act.

Third, inflection moments require us to balance the needs of the long term (the hour hand), the medium term (the minute hand) and the short term (the second hand). It requires thinking across time horizons and building a learning agenda that cuts across these various priorities and goals.

Fourth, there are few obvious or 'right' answers for leaders at inflection moments. Remember how outdated our old mental models of leadership are. It requires tapping into our intrinsic (inner) motivation and understanding what deeply drives us and our stakeholders. As we face an inflection moment, we ourselves change, which only creates further instability.

The stakes are high, but if we can successfully navigate such moments, there's a huge prize ahead: we can futureproof our success.

By building a long-term vision and purpose that builds better lives for us all.

The focus of my work is now squarely on supporting leaders and organisations to successfully navigate these inflection moments and, by doing so, to futureproof their success.

Using the watch analogy, we'll harness a framework for doing this called DIAL:

- Dare a new direction (the hour hand)
- Ignite potential within ourselves and others (the minute hand)
- Align motivations of key stakeholders (the second hand)
- Learn to learn (the watch dial)
- Each part of this book is dedicated to an element of the DIAL framework.

- In every section, we'll explore what each of these mean in detail and how they can come together to provide you with the tools to navigate your own leadership journey.

I hope this book helps you to take fundamental control of your own inflection moments and futureproof your success.

Reflective Questions from Section 1 (Recognising Our Leadership Inflection Moments):

1. *If you and your organisation kept going on your current track, where would you end up five years from now? What about 10 years from now? What would that feel like?*

2. *What mental models about leadership do you carry? Which ones are past their sell-by date and need to be replaced?*

3. *What are your asteroids (external events that affect your organisation and sector)? What changes are happening within your own starship (your organisation and within yourself as a leader)? What does this combination of asteroids and starships mean for the period ahead?*

4. *How can you harness the harsh finality of time to motivate you at these inflection moments?*

5. *What might make your own leadership inflection moments challenging to navigate?*

DIAL FRAMEWORK RECAP:

Dare a new direction (the hour hand)

Ignite potential in ourselves and others (the minute hand)

Align motivations (the second hand)

Learn to learn (the watch dial)

SECTION 2:

THE HOUR HAND:
DARE A NEW DIRECTION

---

*I*n Section 1, we looked at what inflection moments are, why they are so important, and how we can intentionally recognise and respond to them. We also looked at the DIAL framework and how we can balance long-term, medium-term, short-term and overall learning perspectives.

In Section 2, we'll focus on the long-term – daring a new direction. We'll look at why setting a fresh, authentic and distinctive direction is so critical – and why that direction needs to be deeply grounded from within us while employing a sharp and unique perspective on the wider problem at hand. We'll consider how we can offload some of our 'baggage' in terms of expectations and avoid succumbing to traditional thinking in areas like corporate strategy. We'll explore how we can get lost in the problem at hand, so that we become less self-conscious as leaders and avoid issues like impostor syndrome. Finally, we'll look at the power of our perspective to bring others in to help shape our efforts, using the powerful tool of a perspective statement.

In this part of the book, we'll cover the following micro-chapters:

- A Fresh Perspective: Daring to Challenge the Status Quo
- Are You Playing Not to Lose? Knowing When to Dare Again
- Expectation Triangles: The Courage to Make Your Own Choices
- Resist the Strategy Temptress: Be Driven by Direction
- Air Games and Ground Games: Letting Go of Leadership Posturing
- A Genuine Self-Portrait: Finding Our Direction from Within
- Leading = Surfing: Letting Go in the Choppy Waters of Leadership
- Gin and Tonic Leadership: The Importance of Solving Deeply Human Problems
- Reinventing the Peter Principle: The Dangers of Losing Our Small 'p' Purpose

- The Knife of Insight: The Importance of Having a Sharp Leadership Perspective in a Complex System

- Courage or Ruthlessness: Anchoring Ourselves with a Perspective Statement

- Starting from Within: Perspective and Our Career Choices

6: A Fresh Perspective: Daring to Challenge the Status Quo

They say power corrupts. But I think a lack of perspective is even more corrupting because it creates the illusion that we never have to change. It is deeply dishonest.

In La Prisonniere, Marcel Proust wrote: 'The real voyage of discovery consists not in seeking new landscapes but in having new eyes.'

I often work with freshly-minted CEOs or leaders. They arrive with new eyes and energy, eager to bring fresh perspectives to their role from their past voyages.

But they find it hard to acknowledge the elephants in their new rooms.

They want to be bold, but they are afraid of rocking the boat too early. It's natural and understandable. But what so often happens is that they hesitate or wait too long to act.

In short, they go native. In their effort to integrate into their new surroundings, their eyes quickly lose the freshness that compelled them to lead in the first place.

What's always drawn me to David Hockney is how he brings a fresh perspective to every piece, even while capturing landscapes he is deeply familiar with.

The winding vistas in a wood, the Yorkshire Dales or a Californian desert road … Each time the perspective feels bracing and new.

But this playfulness with perspective is also true within a singular Hockney masterpiece.

Recently, I noticed how each panel in a Hockney multimedia installation was taken from a different perspective. The effect is harmonious when you look at it from a distance, but jarring when you look more closely. It's almost as if the artist is consciously seeking to keep us off balance.

In the same way, leaders – whether new or existing – need to balance the best of the existing and the new in how they put forth their perspective. They must find an undiscovered path that can blend both successfully.

They need to acknowledge the best of what has gotten their organisation to this point. To not do so would be deeply disrespectful to their people, those who have put in so much of their blood, sweat and tears. (This is precisely why so much of the 'disruptor' narrative – particularly common in the tech sector – sounds jarring to many ears.)

But the best leaders can speak from both sides of their mouth. They can acknowledge the legacy of a past leadership while being equally honest that a new and fresh perspective is essential when tackling the road ahead.

As leaders, and like Hockney, we may want to keep the people we lead a little off balance.

Not with some Machiavellian intent, but to enable our people to see the deeply familiar with new eyes so they truly want to go on the next voyage of discovery with us.

Leaders, in short, must acknowledge – to themselves and their people – that their organisation is at an inflection moment.

And at inflection moments (unlike in steady-state moments), the cost of inaction is greater than the cost of action.

Don't try to hide or mask the moment you are in; embrace it. And inflect.

7: Are You Playing Not to Lose? Knowing When to Dare Again

Have you ever lost after being massively ahead?

A tennis nut myself, I've lost matches from a set and 5-2 up.

And I've watched the GOAT (greatest of all time) Roger Federer lose to Novak Djokovic in similar positions. So, I'm consoled that it can happen to the best of us.

Then think of companies like Blockbuster and Kodak Print that squandered their huge market leads to what were then tiny disruptors like Netflix and Fuji.

Here's the irony: we can lead patiently, diligently and intentionally over years, even decades. That cumulative success often pays off.

But then, sometimes out of nowhere, we face our moment of truth. As we've seen, that's the core of an inflection moment.

The moment when – as we may or may not remember from our school geometry – the angle of ascent dramatically shifts.

Inflection moments are so tricky because they require us to quickly rewrite the rules that got us to that very point of success. To realise that what has worked unfailingly for so many years is unlikely to get us to where we need to go next.

These moments force us to stop in our tracks and dare to head in a more ambitious direction, all while the stakes are higher than they've ever been.

Facing our inflection moments as leaders takes courage and conviction.

As we've seen, navigating inflection moments requires us to balance the hour hand (long term), minute hand (medium term) and second hand (short term) all at once, precisely when time – unnervingly – seems to stand still as the crisis takes hold. The stress and unpredictability of a situation like this can be deeply daunting.

But we can learn to face down these moments powerfully and emerge even stronger as leaders and people in the process.

I will forever be a Federer fan, but I'll never forget how Djokovic ripped out a forehand winner as he faced down match point in their US Open semi-final epic in 2011. The great Swiss, by contrast, played cautiously in that moment. And that turned the whole match in the Serb's favour.

In this way, inflection moments can also be an opportunity to seize success from the jaws of impending crisis, if only we face them well.

More than anything, the people we lead deserve honesty from us as leaders – our fresh perspective on what the problems are and what needs to change.

Our leadership power today comes much more from this unique value we can bring and less from formal power or authority.

Let's embrace perspective as the fundamental pillar that leadership now rests on.

8: Expectation Triangles: The Courage to Make Your Own Choices

Have you ever got caught in a love triangle? OK. I won't ask you to answer that publicly!

But I see so many leaders getting caught in an equally painful expectations triangle, trying to balance their needs, their company's needs and the needs of those in their personal life. And that's why our backpacks – the load we carry as leaders, mentally, emotionally and practically – can feel so heavy.

The weight often comes from other people – the demands or expectations of a parent, a friend or a spouse in our personal lives. Or from the expectations of our colleagues and the culture around us.

I can guarantee you two things if you ever get caught up in trying to fulfil others' expectations.

First, it will be a game that only escalates in difficulty. When you fulfil one expectation, another even bigger one will quickly come hurtling along.

Second, you will never be enough.

Other people's expectations tend to be based on an 'escalator' model of success: that our lives should progress in a straight and steady upward path. Closely linked to this is a 'should' mindset that suggests there is a certain way of doing things. This is inevitably driven by peer comparison and status.

A female student on the MBA programme I developed at Oxford University's Saïd Business School once told me about the expectations her husband had placed on her – both in terms of salary and prestige. None of these were explicit but, rather, felt like they were hanging in the air. This, in turn, prevented her from exploring the career options that really motivated her. But having a deep conversation with her husband was transformational.

That's a hopeful story. But, sometimes, mental models can leave another person – despite deeply caring about you at their core – unable to 'see' who you truly are anymore.

I once talked to a man in his 40s who had spent two decades grinding through a well-paid and stable career that he didn't find fulfilling in order to meet his family's expectations.

Then he had a midlife epiphany: he wanted to live the next chapter of his work life very differently, setting up a furniture business as an entrepreneur.

He told his wife, who was very supportive, excited and perhaps a little anxious in equal measure. She passed on the news to her father.

At a family lunch a few days later, the man's father-in-law took him aside. He told him that work was meant to be awful. He told him to stop daydreaming and man up.

In a few seconds, the weeks of reinventing and reimagining were over.

If you're caught in an expectations triangle, try to talk to the people who really matter in your life. Explain why the choices ahead mean so much to you and why you feel trapped in the triangle. Remind them that their love and care should be for you in the broadest sense.

And remind them that they loved, married or befriended you for something more constant and eternal – not the exact status or position you have right now.

That you are a living, breathing, evolving being. Not a statue that gathers dust.

9: Resist the Strategy Temptress: Be Driven by Direction

Beware strategy – that seductive temptress. She'll whisper sweet nothings in your ear.

But much of the time they're just saccharine. They have no sustenance.

In Chapter 2, we saw how the situations – authenticity – traits (SAT) triangle can trap us in outdated mental models as leaders and stop us from making a genuine difference to the lives of others.

But, just as tellingly, I find that leaders' backpacks – or Samsonites or TUMIs – are far too heavy these days. Leaders literally feel weighed down. And the biggest weight is often around strategy.

As a former (and proud) strategy consultant myself, I think it's because strategy has too often devolved from being a highly creative, almost artisanal exploration to an industrial, paint-by-numbers process.

I ask so many leaders – across sectors – what their 'strategy' is, and they often churn out a set of targets and growth ambitions.

Strategy tends to be outside-in, meaning it looks externally and dispassionately at the opportunity and then it figures out the most attractive play to make.

But leadership, at its best, is all about what's within – passion, purpose (big 'P' and small 'p'), courage and conviction.

People want to be led by leaders with a vision, not by numbers on PowerPoint slides.

As we'll explore in the coming micro-chapters, I think that direction can be a more helpful bedfellow than strategy today.

Direction, by comparison, starts inside-out – by first asking what deeply drives the leader. It asks what their intrinsic (inner) motivations are and what their unique perspective on the problem is.

But then it quickly moves outside-in – asking the leader to get lost in the problem at hand and in the needs of the people they are serving. Lost to the point that they no longer see themselves. So that they, as a leader, become submerged in something far bigger and far more important.

Because of this constant interplay between inside-out and outside-in thinking, navigating a direction – as opposed to setting strategy – is deeply human, messy, humbling and scary.

My son has just started secondary school, and I am already encouraging him to start packing smaller backpacks. Carrying too much will only slow him down.

Leaders – is it finally time for a little less strategy and a lot more direction?

10: Air Games and Ground Games: Letting Go of Leadership Posturing

Have you ever felt naked as a leader?

As a strategy consultant, I used to feel naked without my PowerPoint slides. Not just naked. Empty. Utterly exposed.

Without the slides, I simply didn't feel 'branded' enough.

I needed my former firm's fancy reputation to justify my expensive billing rate. To feel enough.

It's a pattern that has recurred throughout my life. Even recently, as a newly-minted author, I'd take copies of my book with me to every meeting.

This was all to show people: I am the expert. I know what I am doing. I really have done the work. I was playing the air game. Not the hot air game (though there was some of that too).

The air game is all about leaders showing they are in control.

They try to chair a meeting decisively and authoritatively. They have no qualms telling people what to do or letting them know when they've disappointed them with their performance. (There are better ways to nurture excellence, as we'll explore in subsequent micro-chapters.)

Ironically, this behaviour doesn't demonstrate control and expertise. It demonstrates a lack of confidence in their innate abilities and a focus on retaining power rather their true mission – to help those they are leading. So many Westminster MPs tell me about meetings – at a select committee, for example – where the person leading 'plays' chair. They do the gravitas thing, the authority thing – but there isn't any real substance underneath it.

What almost always happens is this: the air game becomes ever airier (ever fancier slides, ever loftier jargon and ever more elaborate visuals). A vicious cycle.

As this vicious cycle turns, it fosters a growing disconnect with the ground game: the day-to-day reality of the customer, client, community, citizen, patient or student – the person the leader is actually trying to serve.

And that, in turn, often creates an inflection moment.

This might present as partners or customers reluctantly deserting the organisation, or staff leaving because they can't see the connection between their on-the-ground work and the air game their leaders are pontificating about.

When we get into inflection moments like this, the only way forward is to reconnect the air game with the ground game.

Get out of your fancy office. See the realities of the people you are helping and serving with fresh and honest eyes. Spend time with them and particularly with your teams on the ground. Remember that your role as a leader is to empower and serve them. Not the other way around.

Effective leadership is all about being deeply orientated in the ground game and, from that stance, developing a meaningful perspective. The air game is a folly – our egos and our distance from the ground tear us away from the real work.

I have learned that feeling naked is no bad thing for a leader.

Because the alternative is to end up wearing the emperor's new clothes.

11: A Genuine Self-Portrait: Finding Our Direction from Within

When you look in the mirror, what do you see? Do you feel like you're playing it safe?

Do you feel you've compromised? And, by that, I mean on what you haven't done rather than on what you're doing.

I just went to see a retrospective of the American painter Alice Neel at the Barbican Centre. Neel describes herself as a 'collector of souls', painting marginalised figures from eccentrics to labour leaders.

Neel learnt to love the canvas for its ability to bestow truth and conviction.

But so many leaders feel constrained by the canvas – the way they present themselves to their organisation and to the world. It's as if they need to artificially dress up their own presence in the portrait so that the rest of the painting feels far less unique.

Rather than undertake a genuine self-portrait, therefore, they feel compelled to wear the mask of leadership. Hiding behind titles, authority and existing playbooks feels comforting, after all. It can make us feel safer, like wearing armour going into battle. It gives us the illusion of power and control. And it means you don't need to share what you really think – let alone feel.

There are good reasons for this cautious behaviour. Leaders are responsible for other people. They often need to draw in resources – investment or funding – just to make the payroll each month. They need to align different stakeholders – from investors to employees – while still moving forward. It's not an easy balance.

When I was running an organisation in India and Africa, I was acutely aware that each of my employees probably had 20 family members who were, in turn, dependent on them. It was a heavy weight on my shoulders.

But we now know that the best way to achieve success as a leader is not just to make your organisation a little better than another. That's a surefire path to stagnation in an increasingly crowded and competitive world.

The answer is to stand out, to be different, to be distinctive. And also to be genuinely human and vulnerable when you need to. When you do so, others will feel excited to come on board with you.

But how do we gain the courage to do that? Showing our true selves in such a high-stakes situation will surely make us vulnerable?

The good news is that most of the time we already have a strong sense of where we want to go. It's ever present in the back of our minds.

The trick is to let that intrinsic (inner) direction percolate. And then to pour it out when it's piping hot.

I've worked with dozens of leaders, and I usually start with a simple question: 'Imagine you never had to worry about money or resources again. Where would you take your organisation?'

It's a hypothetical question, but the thinking process frees up so much creative energy. And that's because there is almost always a way to get to that path, even if it involves getting there in small, incremental steps.

It's all about embracing the blank canvas of leadership with the freshness and excitement that Alice Neel did. Confronting ourselves with a genuine self-portrait.

And when we do that, there can be no excuses or masks.

Embracing the freedom to be this honest and unvarnished – to be the leader we really think we need to be – is both exhilarating and a little terrifying.

When I visited the exhibition, I noticed two distinct stages of Neel's life. The second stage was so much more expressive. The colours in that final period were bolder and more radiant and the backdrops more immersive.

It turned out that, towards the end of Neel's life, she had been seeing a therapist. He encouraged her to be bolder and more ambitious in her work. To free herself. (We'll explore what authenticity might really mean as a leader in subsequent micro-chapters.)

Whether we are artists or leaders, perhaps it's inevitable that we play a little cautiously in our first chapter.

The key, however, is not to leave our second chapter too late.

12: Leading = Surfing: Letting Go in the Choppy Waters of Leadership

Each morning, a few years ago, I saw a wonderful view from a Cornish cottage in a brief respite between lockdowns.

Each morning I saw the surfers come out.

Their wetsuits served as their single defence against the freezing Atlantic waters. But it was their sheer openness to the waves that I noticed most.

They didn't try and control the thundering water around them. In fact, they knew they couldn't control it.

They had to embrace the waves – both their danger and their majesty – for what they were. They had to surrender themselves and learn to feel the cold of the water and the pull of the currents.

As leaders today, we regularly get thrust into the towering waves and icy currents of the challenge at hand. Often with only a fig leaf of a wetsuit for protection, if we're lucky.

Overwhelmed, we often try to fight against them, to ignore how powerful they are. The end result? We end up dithering, grandstanding and/or gaming – basically treading water.

What I learned from the surfers that week was just to let go and embrace the waves. We can acknowledge the bumpy conditions we are leading within and try to work with them, however scary that might be.

If we can do that, we lose our self-consciousness and, with it, feelings like impostor syndrome.

We stop trying to become the leader we have seen other people be, or what we have seen in television shows. (And, also, the leader we think we should be.)

In fact, we don't even think about leadership at all.

We just get lost in the currents and lead because ... well, we have no choice but to do so.

We dissolve into the waves like the surfers do. And we do whatever we need to do – float, paddle, swim – to keep afloat and truly make a difference to the lives of others.

As we've seen in previous micro-chapters, leading is not about having a predetermined playbook for every situation, being irresistibly authentic or having a perfect set of leadership traits. Nor is it (especially today) about formal power and position.

It's all about getting lost in something bigger than ourselves.

It's about seeing – and having the courage to seize – inflection moments for what they truly are.

But it's also about letting go and trusting our ability to navigate the choppy waters when these moments arise. It's about forgetting ourselves and simply doing what the waves and currents need us to do.

In essence, I wonder if we have obsessed far too much about the myth and cult of leadership (the noun). I believe we need to focus much more on leading (the verb).

Those valiant souls I saw in Cornwall would call themselves surfers (the noun) for sure.

But, more than anything, what I saw each morning was the simple beauty of the verb. They were surfing. So, perhaps the equation should actually read: leading = surfing

So, wanna go catch some waves?

13: Gin and Tonic Leadership: The Importance of Solving Our Deeply Human Problems

What do gin and tonics have to do with leadership? Much more than you might think.

Leaders today essentially face two types of problems.

Wicked problems are messy, intractable human problems. They relate to us as individuals and to society and thus there are no easy or stable solutions. Human motivations, behaviour and interdependence are at the core of what makes a problem wicked. We are unpredictable and incredibly complex.

They're like the best gin: punchy and complex, full of far-flung botanicals and often with a surprising final note.

But ingesting too much, or too quickly, can also leave us feeling intoxicated, even drunk. They are the sort of problems that can leave us reeling as leaders.

Kind problems, by contrast, are more stable. They relate to everything that is not human, so they are infinitely more simple. There is usually a technical solution that can address the issue at hand. They're like the tonic in our G&T.

The challenges that leaders face today are invariably a wicked/kind cocktail. But while we often coast through the kind problems, we can be stymied by the complexity of the wicked problems while overlooking their importance.

Take the pandemic and the challenges our national leaders faced in steering us through these unchartered waters. The kind aspect of the problem (the vaccine) was something that we did remarkably well as a species, producing it in record time.

But the wicked problem of how we organise society and our economy through a pandemic, from social distancing to lockdowns to furlough schemes, was often wildly reactive, with decisions taken on the hoof. It's unclear that any country – whether it was China or Sweden, or anywhere in between these two extremes – did this particularly well.

Or take leadership in the tech industry. We've seen massive shifts in our ability to connect with people around the world (built on kind innovations in social media). But we've put much less thought into the wicked ramifications of this increased connection, from screen addiction to comparison culture to the subversion of democracies.

I see this temptation in leaders today to focus on the kind elements of their role, hoping they can wish away the less appealing wicked elements.

It's understandable. But it's unwise.

Because no matter how good the tonic is, it's only when the gin kicks in that leadership truly packs a punch.

As any good bartender will tell you, a good G&T is usually one quarter gin and three quarters tonic. That's also a pretty accurate ratio of how most leaders currently spend their time: three quarters on kind problems and a quarter on the wicked.

In many ways, that makes sense. Many aspects of leadership are about driving execution and delivery – accurately, reliably and on time.

But the big societal inflection moments in front of us – from AI to the climate – will deeply shift this ratio. In most of these areas we already have strong technical solutions. It's cooperating with other humans to find a way to get these technical solutions into the world that's going to be the challenge. Inevitably, the wicked element will become ever stronger in the leadership cocktail.

And at inflection moments – those make-or-break points for organisations and leaders – the cocktail becomes stronger still. It's three quarters gin and one quarter tonic.

When they occur, so much of the leadership task is to grapple with existential questions. Where do I play? What difference do I want to make for the people I help and serve? How can I scale and sustain that impact? This is all about finding your big 'P' purpose – a problem bigger than ourselves that will feed and sustain our motivation. This is something I'll explore in more detail in later micro-chapters.

There will be lots of strong cocktails ahead.

The key is to sip bravely – and even enjoy it – without getting too drunk.

14: Reinventing the Peter Principle: The Dangers of Losing Our Small 'p' Purpose

Is the Peter Principle – the idea that our skills and abilities can't keep up as we get promoted to leadership positions – past its sell-by date?

I believe so.

Today, even when leaders are on the headiest of ascents up the career ladder, I rarely see them struggling in terms of their competence.

Developments have come thick and fast in that domain. There's a lot to be grateful for in that news.

For instance, management training has vastly improved. And a stronger – though still imperfect – 360-degree feedback culture means leaders are far more aware of what areas they need to develop. There is also more support available (from technical training to coaching).

What I see instead is another destructive pattern: the leader who suddenly loses their purpose when they step up.

It might be the sales leader who is at their best interfacing with customers, now forced to crunch sales forecasts or negotiate incentive schemes for team members.

Or the teacher or doctor who loves nurturing children or patients, now forced to spend their time reporting for Ofsted or working on NHS waiting list targets.

In all these scenarios, a new leader may be quite capable of executing these responsibilities – their competence is not the issue. But their purpose – small 'p' purpose – is deeply diminished in the process.

I define small 'p' purpose as how our work helps and serves others, each day, every day.

The world doesn't come crashing down in these examples. But their commitment to their career ebbs away a little more each day.

And as employees increasingly bring more of their personal lives to work – while putting up much stronger work-life balance boundaries – empathetic leaders face a double whammy. They feel forced to double down on keeping their teams happy, and they spend less time with the people they are ultimately helping and serving.

I think this is why hundreds of thousands of leaders, at all levels and across sectors, have been leaving our workforce.

My own experience with organisations suggests this problem is even more acute for female leaders.

Female leaders often (unfairly) feel greater pressure to accept leadership roles on the organisation's terms rather than their own. Many of them also find it harder to 'craft' their roles to enable them to still do what they truly love – where they experience flow – or to negotiate aspects that would keep them feeling purposeful. For example, a teacher promoted to the school's leadership team could still spend two days a week teaching a class directly.

This trend is a silent and more insidious killer of leadership potential than the more familiar Peter Principle.

Rather than seeing organisations implode with incompetence, we see their very purpose erode. And this produces a far more lethal blow.

As I've done some fascinating work with philanthropic leaders across Central and Eastern Europe, I'm going to suggest this less acknowledged problem be named so we can start to tackle it head-on:

The Petra Principle.

No offence to either of you, Peter or Petra, but we want to see a lot less of each of you both in the years to come.

15: The Knife of Insight: The Importance of Having a Sharp Leadership Perspective in a Complex System

Which do you trust to build a better world for us all: people or systems?

I see this tension in every domain that I work with leaders in – from corporate life to politics to public sector organisations like the UK's NHS.

In a nutshell, I think we need both, but we need a bridge between the two to ensure that we are leading with real intention in a complex system. And that bridge is perspective.

It's trendy nowadays to talk about systemic approaches and system change, but the truth is that I see a lot of leaders fall victim to system paralysis.

They spend years trying to deeply diagnose the problems within the system around them. Yet, at the end of it, they feel more powerless than when they started because the challenges in the system seem so complex, intertwined and intractable.

What can end up happening then is that we 'go native' in the system that surrounds us. We give in to it, leaning into a kind of learned helplessness and, with it, a hollow system acceptance.

I see that phenomenon right now in the NHS and in politics. So many bright and talented leaders won't question these systems because 'that's just how things are'.

But there's hope.

As we explored in the first micro-chapter in this section, as leaders, perspective is what gives us legitimacy with our people.

A powerful perspective that is grounded, distinctive and authentic enables others to see a system problem with new eyes. It means we don't need to 'push' change on to others. If our people are energised by our perspective, they'll 'pull' us instead. We will end up running behind our people as leaders – guiding them as they build on our perspective at a hundred miles an hour.

Perspective is also like the knife of insight that cuts through the complexities of systems.

A strong perspective statement from a leader can unlock both their own leadership motivation and their ability to see the system's problems differently.

And perspective statements don't have to be final. The best ones have an explorer mindset; they provide a starting point but they also enable leaders – along with the people they lead – to discover and refine their aims and intentions as they go. We'll dive into how to develop perspective statements in the next micro-chapter.

The fundamental truth is that we, as leaders, have more power and autonomy than we often think. The key is to seize it and to take that first step.

If we don't, we will find ourselves paralysed trying to find the perfect or 'right' answer (when perfection doesn't exist). And the systems we operate in will, in turn, be paralysed by our inaction.

I love James Clear's work, captured in his book Atomic Habits. His fundamental insight is that our habits are only as good as the systems we build around them. For example, having a good system where healthy food is always near us will help us stick to a new diet. Unless they are obvious, attractive, easy and satisfying, they won't become habitual.

I think perspective, like habits, can also be atomic.

If we start – however hesitantly – to articulate our perspective, the insight and motivational momentum compounds each day. Every time our perspective shifts, it gives us new energy and insights, and it allows us to see parts of a system afresh. That then allows us to sharpen our existing approach or adopt new ones. It's a virtuous cycle.

As leaders, we need our people and the systems we operate in to rise – not fall – to the level of our perspective.

The first step is to have the courage to articulate our perspective.

16: Courage or Ruthlessness: Anchoring Ourselves with a Perspective Statement

Do I want to lead in the first place? Doesn't being a leader mean being ruthless?

I come across many people with huge potential who never become leaders because of this fear.

Or leaders who jump off the leadership saddle far too early because it's getting too hot, proverbially speaking.

That's why perspective can be such a powerful constant. It can remind us of who we want to be as leaders, rather than what we think we need to be, because it grounds us in how we see a wicked problem differently from others. And, in doing so, it reminds us of the bigger picture – the waves – so that we focus on that rather on ourselves.

I recently spent a week in Morocco visiting my wife's family. Everywhere we went I was served a pot of mint tea.

The temperature had to be just right – neither lukewarm nor scalding.

Perspective statements are similar. They're a simple tool for us to express our unique vantage point as a leader compared to what conventional wisdom dictates. They need to be distinctive and fresh but also aligned at a high level to how others see the problem. They distinguish us and our value.

The best perspective statements encompass:

1. Who really needs to be supported

Often this means going back to redefine 'who' is integral and core to realising your perspective. For instance, if you are leading a bank or a retail business, the store or bank manager is likely to be the 'engine room' of your business. They're the people who should really be there for your customers during their 'moments of truth' i.e. when they are sold a faulty product or are a victim of a fraud (both of which happened to me recently).

2. What really needs to be done to support them

As leaders, we often assume it's us that needs to do more. But many times, leading is about stepping out of the way of those we support. The 'what' may be about letting others around you take responsibility and accountability, aligned to the perspective you set. This is what really makes an organisation futureproof and able to scale. I wish I had been more aware of this truth when I was a CEO.

3. How that needs to be done

Hopefully, we're now clear on who needs to be supported and what we must do (or not do) to support them. Now we need to think about how we do it. In the

34

bank example, it may be about creating alignment and giving our teams the right level of autonomy with some guardrails (something we'll dive more deeply into in subsequent micro-chapters). For example, making sure the branch manager immediately calls a victim of fraud and that they have the time and budget to solve their problem quickly.

If we are clear and rigorous in following our perspective statement, even if that means being tough – and genuinely focus on our mission to serve others and not ourselves – we can afford to be a lot less worried about becoming the proverbial 'ruthless leader'.

On the other hand, if we're doing something because it will make us look good in someone else's eyes (the big boss or our board), then we should be worried.

The line between ruthlessness and courage is a fine one. Like the mint tea in Morocco, leading is about being neither lukewarm nor scalding.

I recently heard Merck executive chairman Kenneth C. Frazier's definition of leadership: making the biggest difference to the largest number. I think, in essence, that's what a perspective statement helps us to do. It keeps us (and the people we lead) truly honest.

So, I think we can agree that leading ≠ ruthlessness. Rather, leading = not being ruthless for its own sake.

17: Starting from Within: Perspective and Our Career Choices

Most of the career advice we give people today is flawed.

And asking people what career they want to be in is the most fatally flawed question of them all.

You may think it's because the majority of jobs people might go into haven't been invented yet. To a certain extent, this is true. A decade ago, who would have ever believed that podcasting and AI prompting would be some of today's hottest careers?

But there's an even bigger problem.

The career advice we usually give is framed around a mindset I call 'career capture'.

Career capture starts with the question: what are the 'hot', lucrative and most feasible careers that I can get in on early? Careers where, if I do get in, I will be propelled on an ever-upward 'escalator path'?

The challenge with career capture is that it often encourages career 'hacking' and 'gaming'. We focus on the shortest possible path to obtain the hot job. But it often doesn't link to our unique perspective on an issue (which we've explored before), or to what drives and motivates us on a deeper level. So, when times get tough (which they inevitably will), we question whether we will persist in these jobs.

And what happens if our job assumptions turn out to be incorrect? Job and career trends are fickle, especially nowadays. AI prompting could be much less 'hot' even next year, especially if user interfaces become simpler. Also, what happens if the 'hot' job doesn't meet our expectations, as the organisational psychologist Adam Grant points out? If the role doesn't align with your interests and strengths, you won't be able to thrive even if there are obvious rewards to be gained.

But what about starting from a different place? What about looking at ourselves first rather than starting with the marketplace? An alternative mindset – 'problem contribution' – starts by asking the question: what are the wicked problems out there that I am deeply fascinated by and want to help solve? (Climate change, AI and the future of work are all great examples of wicked problems). And, importantly, what is my unique perspective on those problems?

Based on that perspective, you will often find many different paths to help solve those wicked problems you are drawn to. It may be as an executive, a consultant, an academic researcher, a journalist or a coach. And that path can shift over time.

For example, you may decide to enter the field of AI through an industry body because your perspective is that AI ethics are falling behind the core technology (which they are). But you may then evolve to become an AI ethics coach or consultant to others as you gain broader experience.

Leadership today is less about your formal role and position. It comes from crafting and refining a unique and authentic perspective on problems that deeply matter to us. And then using that perspective to develop paths towards making that perspective a reality. Paths that will help us to be distinctive, motivated and successful in what we do.

So, don't begin by asking what job or career can do the most for you. Ask instead what problem you can help most to solve.

Reflective Questions from Section 2 (Dare a New Direction)

1. *What is your reflection on the fact that the source of leadership power today comes from having a unique and fresh perspective?*

2. *Is there a wicked problem (or several wicked problems) that you are particularly fascinated by? Ones that you get deeply lost in? What are they? Why? (Please note that these wicked problems can be related or unrelated to your current area of focus).*

3. *Try to write a perspective statement around one of those problems, using the following prompts to structure it:*

    Compared to conventional wisdom, how do you think differently about this problem? Who needs to be engaged and supported, and why?

    What needs to be done, and why?

    How does it need to be done, and why?

4. *What is the new direction that comes out of your perspective? This could be in terms of your existing leadership role and/or in how you think about fashioning your longer-term career.*

5. *How will you align the key people in your life and organisation – from colleagues to family – with your perspective? How can you help them co-create and build on that perspective?*

6. *What expectations will you jettison in order to achieve the above? Key areas to think about are the expectations you have of yourself, others' expectations of you and your expectations around money.*

7. *How will you stay grounded by your small 'p' purpose, and the realities of the people you are ultimately serving, all the way through this?*

DIAL FRAMEWORK RECAP:

Dare a new direction (the hour hand)

Ignite potential in ourselves and others (the minute hand)

Align motivations (the second hand)

Learn to learn (the watch dial)

SECTION 3:

THE MINUTE HAND: IGNITE POTENTIAL IN OURSELVES AND OTHERS

---

*I*n Section 2, we focused on how to dare an exciting new direction, built on the foundation of our unique perspective on the problems we face.

In Section 3, we'll look at how we can nurture our own potential and the potential of others in realising that direction. We'll examine the ground-breaking ACE (authenticity, connection, excellence) as the pillars of potential, and how to balance these pillars for the best effect. We'll look at how we can create cultures where everyone's potential can be nurtured, rather than seeing progress as a zero-sum game. We'll also look at the key barriers to realising potential – from concerns over privilege to the narrow way in which we often currently view diversity – and how to overcome them. We'll also look at how to structure and sequence careers and relationships to maximise the potential in ourselves and others, including through perfecting the art of nurturing, and opening up connections and opportunities. All of this will enable us to harness our and others' potential so that we can achieve the direction we really want.

In this part of the book, we'll cover the following micro-chapters:

- All-In Leading: How to Inspire Others
- Hardball versus Softball: Is There a New Way to Lead?
- Diamond Hunting: Nurturing the Potential We See in Everyone
- The End of the Escalator: Do We Really Need to Play by the Rules?
- Idealist or Realist: The Right Path to Your End Destination
- Lightening Our Privilege Baggage: Focusing on the 99%
- Spotting Potential: Listen to Their Peers
- Shades of Grey: What Authenticity Potential Really Means
- Prizing Open Windows: Revealing Our Hidden Selves
- No Easy Answers: Asking the Right Questions at the Right Time

- The How, Not the What: Originality versus Amplifying
- What Is Diversity? Finding Alignment
- Opportunity Hoarding: Opening Up Our Networks to Pay It Forward
- Run Towards Generosity: Building Networks Founded on Trust, Letting Go and Intentionality
- Access All Areas: Being in The Room Where It Happens
- Helping Those in the Ring: We Must Nurture Potential as Leaders

18: All-In Leading: How to Inspire Others

Are you really an 'all-in leader'?

(Vegetarians and vegans, you may want to skip the next four lines).

The 'all in' option at London chophouse Blacklock is itself a heady all-in experience. Towering racks of beef, pork and lamb sizzle on your plate, with flatbreads chewy and heavy with their cumulative juices. You can't do true justice to the meat without using your hands. I can count several once-white shirts as the casualties of these meals (and, yes, each time it was worth it).

Many CEOs and leaders I talk to lament that their teams are no longer 'all in'. At least not in the same way they were pre-pandemic.

The phenomenon of 'quiet quitting' – those unhappy in their jobs doing the bare minimum rather than leaving their roles altogether – is well documented all over the world.

But that's not all there is to it. There's a leadership elephant in the room that I believe needs to be talked about.

When I'm asked to speak to employees at these same organisations, they tell me that they don't see their leaders being all in either.

Yes, they might see their leaders pound their hours and send emails at all times of the day. Indeed, employees rarely question their leaders' hard graft.

But they do often ask what their leaders stand for on a deeper level.

Employees understand that compromise is part of leadership. But they see their leaders compromise in ways that sometimes feels uncomfortable. For example, putting the need to meet a target or financial metric ahead of what really matters to a customer or citizen. Or advancing a project for short-term status or gain ahead of what's important for the long-term flourishing of the organisation. Or (most commonly) not articulating what really matters to them as individuals – or wearing that leadership mask I've spoken about.

When they feel brave enough to question their leaders at these times, they're told: 'That's just how the system works.' And, of course, they don't dare to question again.

Learned helplessness is also a well-evidenced psychological construct. It's the idea that we can construct and create our own sense of powerlessness based on the signals around us. A powerlessness that is far greater than our reality dictates. The irony is that every CEO wants their employees to feel autonomous. And yet, they often (inadvertently) cling to the fig leaf of learned helplessness themselves.

This creates a vicious cycle: employees see their leaders wear the mask of leadership. So, they put on their quiet-quitting masks.

As we'll explore in the next micro-chapters, truly effective leaders don't just accept 'the system' as it is, for better or worse. They work with their teams – and often external stakeholders and peer organisations – to shape a better system for everyone.

In turn, that better system enables them to truly lead: to inspire and nurture others to reach places they wouldn't have reached otherwise (which is, for me, the most fundamental definition of leadership).

Leaders, here are two questions to ask yourself on a deep level:

- Do the people I lead really know what I stand for?
- Is what I stand for really enough?

Here's the honest truth: if we want our teams to be 'all in' (as we should), we need to lead from within ourselves.

19: Hardball versus Softball: Is There a New Way to Lead?

Do you play hardball or softball?

Be honest: are you a hardball leader? Here's how to diagnose yourself.

Hardball leaders see work, leadership and life as a battle.

They use terms like 'destroy the enemy', 'arming up' and 'fire up the troops' when they communicate with others.

Hardball leaders see a secret weapon in the field of battle: themselves.

Only their unique perspective can win the battle, given the existential threats that they often feel they are dealing with. Though they do acknowledge the importance of loyal troops.

Or are you a softball leader?

Softball leaders prize consensus and harmony at work. They value listening and often use fashionable terms like 'servant leadership' to describe their style.

Let me level with you: I don't think hardball or softball leadership stand much chance of building a better world for us all.

Tide founder George Bevis pointed out to me how the Silicon Valley leadership archetype is extremely hardball. Think Steve Jobs, Jeff Bezos, Mark Zuckerberg and Elon Musk.

Yes, these companies have been wildly successful financially (at least most of the time). But most of us would agree that their impact on our world has been mixed.

I have been investigating the culture in UK politics recently, across parties. What I've seen is more resolutely hardball than anything Silicon Valley can serve up. And, yes, the impact on our country also feels decidedly mixed.

But softball doesn't quite cut it either.

I have watched many softball leaders bite the dust because they weren't tough or resilient enough to stay the course.

My 11-year-old plays cricket, and two years ago he made the transition to hardball cricket. The England and Wales Cricket Board (ECB) did a good job of managing that transition. They made him play with a 'hard' soft ball for a full 18 months beforehand. And then they made sure he learned to put on his pads and helmet correctly. But (critically) they still ensured he got to transition to a hard ball at the right playing age.

Let's face it: life is often hardball.

The best leaders I work with fully acknowledge that. But they create cultures in their teams that feel more soft hardball and (when possible) even softball. And they protect their teams with pads and helmets when the quickest deliveries and meanest bouncers are bowled.

That often means sticking their neck out when someone else – usually more senior – doesn't treat someone in their team in the right way.

Or it might mean 'going into bat' for someone by recommending them for a promotion or new opportunity, even when others don't quite see their potential and want to play it safe.

They are willing to take risks and, where needed, put themselves on the line.

The very best leaders go even further. They stand right by their teams when the most ferocious balls come at them. They protect them, personally fending off the most dangerous ones.

So, there is an element of personal risk and danger in being a real leader today. And, at many levels, that's a huge shame. But it's part of a leader's duty to pay it forward. And they can do this knowing that, gently and gradually, making their voices heard can help change the rules of the game.

Yes, life is often hardball.

But that doesn't mean we need to be hardball leaders.

When I ask the UK politicians I am interviewing if they would want their own children to enter politics, there is a resounding consensus: no.

The risk of hardball leadership is not just its very mixed results in the present. It's that, in the future, our very best talent will simply refuse to play.

20: Diamond Hunting: Nurturing the Potential We See in Everyone

Are you a great screener of talent?

Or a world-class nurturer of potential? As leaders, we need to be both.

But I would argue that we have spent too much time and effort trying to 'objectively' and 'rigorously' screen for talent.

All in the often futile hope of finding that previously undiscovered fully-formed gem.

And we've spent too little effort nurturing that gem to reach its true potential: a diamond.

This approach is endemic in our society. It's how top universities and schools select students, how sporting teams pick athletes, how venture capitalists (VCs) screen entrepreneurs to fund, how political parties select candidates … the list goes on.

There's a deep irony here. In every sector today, we want to increase the proportion of people from underrepresented backgrounds.

This is absolutely the right goal, but that takes real nurturing. If we don't provide that, we may attract new groups of people, but on a false promise. We will leave them stranded so they plateau or even fail outright.

So, why do we always look for the final product and not the diamond in the rough? The truth is that nurturing potential is tough. It takes time, and often it feels thankless.

In the next section of the book, I want to recast nurturing as essentially a heroic activity and the most fundamental characteristic of leadership.

Because only screening for talent is an abdication of leadership responsibility.

Talent is innate. It requires nothing of us, beyond just picking the best of what is already there.

Potential is forward looking. It requires work, but the long-term rewards for us and our people can be so much greater.

That's why inflection moments can be such powerful tools for us as leaders – and why they can allow us to shine. They enable us – even force us – to ensure that we bring everyone's potential to the challenge at hand. Because the urgency of the inflection moment demands nothing less.

Here's the tough truth: talent is 'innate', but only up to a point. Our success deeply reflects our advantages and the luck of the draw.

I remember visiting a tiny tennis club in Split, Croatia, that had created several Wimbledon champions. Those champions were innately 'talented' for sure. But they had a huge advantage – proximity to a remarkable coach and an excellent facility on their doorstep.

It is often said that talent is evenly distributed, while opportunity is not.

Yet the very promise of 'opportunity' is only real if there is nurturing of potential alongside it. Otherwise, there's just the illusion of the open door, which quickly slams shut.

The key to being a great nurturer, as we'll explore in the next micro-chapters, is to resist the seductive illusion that selection of talent is the be-all and end-all. No matter how 'rigorously' we select someone, there is inherent (unintended) bias involved. Study after study shows that we tend to hire people that look and sound like ourselves.

The real trick is to create cultures that truly nurture the potential of all.

It's a big ambition, but it can be done. It requires an abundance mindset around potential and not the scarcity mindset that screening talent usually employs.

There's nothing more noble that we can do as leaders than to see the potential in all.

Because if we can pull it off, we will truly enable our people to break free of their past as they leap into their future.

21: The End of the Escalator: Do We Really Need to Play by the Rules?

Deference. Respect for authority. Do these inspire or inhibit potential?

As an immigrant of Asian descent, this question has always been a challenging one for me personally.

The notion of playing by the rules was deeply ingrained in my own childhood. I can remember numerous conversations with my parents (often as we were driving somewhere) when they reminded me how important this was to becoming successful.

It remains as vivid in my mind as the mythical comics I would read during my summers in India or the fairy tales of my youth like Hansel and Gretel.

It took me a long time – late into my twenties – to realise that's all it was. A myth and a fairy tale.

Because implicit in the 'playing by the rules' mindset is the 'escalator' view of success: if you play by the rules, everyone will keep marching up the escalator. Essentially, if we respect the system, we will be rewarded fairly and eventually reach the top.

What I eventually understood was that while the escalator does generally move up (most of the time, for most people), it does so at wildly different speeds and heights depending on who you are. The system is rigged.

Our real leadership power comes not from trying to climb faster – or overtaking others up the stairs – but from influencing the speed and height of the escalator itself. By changing the system so more people can rise to the top and become leaders.

I increasingly think of nurturing potential as a balancing act.

We do need to get onto the escalator in the first place – perhaps even cling to the handrail, as most immigrants have had to do – but this alone leaves far too many behind.

Once we're firmly on, we still need to keep climbing, but we also need to focus on influencing the overall trajectory.

We can do that in how we ascend. We can show that other (our own) ways of doing things are just as effective as 'playing by the rules'. We can be louder or quieter about this, but the honest truth is that people will pay far more heed to what we do rather than what we say.

But we can also do it by making space for others to climb in the ways they see fit.

The 'my way or the highway' approach to defining potential will limit others who are climbing below you. And it will limit you in the process. All because it takes such a narrow view of what success and potential looks like, and it doesn't see you – or the other person – as real, genuine and unique human beings.

I remember leaving a job because of a manager who didn't 'see' me as a person. He only saw a version of himself that he wanted me to be. And that wasn't who I was, even though I had myriad other strengths that were actually very complementary to his. To leave a job because someone cannot see your true potential is a huge loss, in addition to the emotional scarring it created (for me and perhaps for him too).

The higher up the escalator you go, the dizzier you can feel. At this point, it may make sense to spend less time climbing (because you are already very high up) and more time influencing the slope of the stairs below you. It's recognising that while you've climbed to (or close to) the top, you did it with lots of advantages that others beneath you perhaps don't have. So, now it's time to make the ascent fairer for everyone.

There is something deeply appealing about the escalator model. For immigrants (like my parents) who came to the UK from a more chaotic India, it offered hope of stability and betterment. Of eventual success. Perhaps even a dose of salvation.

But it can be an extremely dangerous myth, as damaging as the fallacy (that still persists in many sectors) that people of Asian or minority descent are hard workers and good followers but not great leaders. (Thankfully, a slew of corporate CEOs and even prime ministers are dispelling that myth.)

The escalator model is so dangerous because it assumes there are gracious grown-ups who are navigating the escalator and treating everyone on it fairly and equally.

Here's the truth for those who are not: we are the real grown-ups now, and we don't need your escalator.

22: Idealist or Realist: The Right Path to Your End Destination

Are you a 'follow your passion now' idealist?

Or are you a 'build the right foundations first' realist?

When someone asks for career advice, which way do you counsel them?

The question from your mentee or from someone you know who's early in their career is usually couched as some variant of the following:

Should I go and work on my passion (whether that's a start-up idea, a social enterprise, a creative career or self-employment) right away? Because I am truly excited about it.

Or

Should I build the right 'stepping stones' towards that path first? (For example, work for a consulting firm, a bank or a large media agency?) Because I worry that I don't have the foundational skills I need yet.

This latter option is often known as the deferred life plan.

I often find myself veering between these two states – idealist and realist – when these conversations arise. Often my answer is based on my perception of the person and (if I'm being very honest) my mood that day.

To be a strong and authentic nurturer of potential, however, I think we (and I) need a more systematic way of approaching this 'deferred life plan' question.

It has been a big theme of the programmes I've been teaching at Saïd Business School at the University of Oxford and at Homerton College at the University of Cambridge.

It's also something I've grappled with in my own life. During the first 10 years of my career, I took a mixture of safer paths – consulting, tech and then undertaking an MBA – before embarking on a 15-year rollercoaster ride, first as a social entrepreneur and now as a leadership advisor.

Along the way, however, I met inspiring and successful social entrepreneurs, like John Rendel of PEAS and George Srour of Building Tomorrow, who pursued their paths pretty much straight from college.

So, which is the better path?

I think there is some nuance in these results which can guide us as to how to make this decision. Here are five guiding questions for ourselves – or others – in considering this trade-off:

1. Am I absolutely sure there is not a direct path to my passion project now?

There are many more career options and pathways now than ever before. In certain circumstances, there may not be a big trade-off in starting your passion project straight away. For example, Inès Magré told me about a new programme that pairs fresh graduates with start-up founders and provides leadership development training. If you're a young leader who is passionate about entrepreneurship, what a great win-win – jumping into what you love without sacrificing structure, networks and support.

2. Is the deferred life plan really a stepping stone?

Will it help me build transferable skills, experiences and credibility that will help me towards my ultimate goal? How will it contribute in other ways? For example, will it give me the financial freedom to take risks later on? Will it develop useful networks? And will I lose any first mover advantage by delaying jumping into a new field while it's in its formative stages?

3. Will I be 'all in' while pursuing the stepping stone?

You can only transfer value from a stepping stone career if you're committed to it, you learn along the way and you have an impact. You don't want to be 'ghosting' your way through, as you won't grow. Is there enough in the deferred path to keep you motivated?

4. Do I have a 'stepping off' point and a forcing mechanism?

The longer we pursue a stepping stone career, the harder it can become to step off the rocks into the choppier waters of our passion project. As financial rewards and status accumulate, they become hardwired into our lifestyle and identity. That's why having a forcing mechanism helps. I've always admired Ashish Dhawan for committing to leave his successful private equity career at the age of 40 to make a difference in education. And, like clockwork, on his 40th birthday, he did just that.

5. Will I have time to explore my long-term direction while I pursue my stepping stone?

As Herminia Ibarra, professor of organisational behaviour at London Business School, has shown in her research, career change is about acting into new ways of thinking and not thinking into new ways of acting. By taking on tangible roles and projects – a board seat or a volunteer position perhaps – that can help us experiment within and explore the area of our passion project, we will start to develop the mindset we need to succeed within it.

In all of these questions, we need to remember that life is both long and short.

Yes, some of us may live to 100. But within that, remember we may only have 100,000 working hours.

Each hour not doing what we love can add up fast, so be careful not to dally too long. The cost of inaction can exceed the cost of action.

I agree that the deferred life plan can often be a smart, strategic and safer choice. But it shouldn't be an excuse to not ultimately do what we are really here to do.

Our ultimate destination – that which lights a fire within us – should always be in our sights. It's just that there are different ways of getting there. And if we choose stepping stones, it may taste even sweeter when we reach it.

23: Lightening Our Privilege Baggage: Focusing on the 99%

A CEO I work with calls me a 'walking 1%'.

He's referring to my educational privilege – my degrees from the University of Cambridge, the University of Oxford and INSEAD.

Like many leaders, I struggle with privilege. Because I have always felt that so many other people had just as much potential as me, but they didn't have the opportunities I had.

Here are the five things I've learned about this thorny area (in case you're grappling with similar questions).

1. Acknowledge it

I could kid myself that my good fortune is the result of me rising in a 'meritocracy'. There's a tiny bit of truth in that. I did work hard. But I've learned to face a deeper truth: I was the fortunate beneficiary of what Warren Edward Buffett calls the 'ovarian lottery' (a supportive, stable, educated home). By accepting that, we can be more open and empathetic to other people and why they may not be as polished as us, or rough around their proverbial edges. That doesn't mean they didn't have potential; they just lacked the same opportunities to realise it.

2. Embrace your choices

Most of us grew up in a 'winner takes all' educational system and economy. That system has a clear goal – for individuals to amass as much status and wealth as quickly as possible. As leaders now, we can continue that approach, or we can embrace the relative 'cushion' that our privilege has given us and use it to take a different path. We can define what 'enough' means for us. Once we've achieved that, we can then devote our lives to what matters to us rather than chasing these outward signs of power. Most people don't have that choice, so why not embrace ours?

3. Find your big 'P' purpose if you can

I define purpose (big 'P' purpose) as getting lost in a wicked problem that's bigger than us. This might be climate change, inequality, diversity or the future of work, health or education reform – problems that are messy, intractable and human, with no easy solutions. The point is not that you are going to brilliantly and heroically 'solve' these problems (because wicked problems can never fully be solved). However, you can make a meaningful contribution, and you will rarely wake up wondering what it is you bring to the world. Not everyone has the chance to take something like this on (I had a very supportive wife and family). But if you do, take it. It's a way to recognise your privilege and give back.

4. Embed small 'p' purpose in everything you do (with no excuses)

Whatever you do for a living, you can find a way to help and serve others each and every day. You can do that in how you smile at the cleaner in the office. Or in whether you genuinely put the needs of your team member or customer first. Most of all, you can proactively help people who are not in your direct social networks. If a client asks you for an internship for their son or daughter, you may well say yes. But you could also take this opportunity to create another internship designed for those who have not had the same advantages – and you can encourage your client to do the same in their organisation. In doing this, we can try to change the system of privilege from the inside.

5. Parent differently

Many of us had (well-meaning) parents who told us it was a 'dog eat dog' world out there. They fed us the idea of a zero-sum game of life where there are only winners and losers. But the economic evidence and our own experience tells us the opposite – that we flourish by nurturing the potential of others. Let's change how we talk to our own kids. If we don't, we'll just pass on this system of privilege and the associated guilt for generations.

So, yes, I have come to accept being a walking 1%.

But I've also learned the best way of dealing with privilege. It's to focus on the 99%.

24: Spotting Potential: Listen to Their Peers

How do you spot potential in a person?

I recently watched the wonderful movie Air starring Matt Damon and Ben Affleck.

It's the story of how the brand Nike was reborn in its early days by taking a chance on a new direction. All through nurturing the potential of one athlete: Michael Jordan.

The choice of Jordan was itself inspired. Nike managers were intrigued that Jordan's teammates always looked so relaxed when it was his turn to shoot. Even at the most critical and challenging moments.

There is a powerful insight in there: the best way to spot potential is to gauge that person's reputation among their peers.

There is a lot of 'kiss up, kick down' behaviour in work cultures today. That means it's hard to gauge how someone you are hiring really thinks and behaves.

And no matter how elaborate your selection system is – how many tests or interviews you employ – these systems can always be gamed. So, treat information you gain from these with caution.

Rather than relying on these systems, trust the people who have been in the real game with that person (literally and metaphorically). It's the day-to-day behaviour of someone that really counts.

So, when you try to spot potential, don't just trust your own judgment, seek out the judgment of others. Even with the best intentions, we all have blind spots.

Trust your networks (that's why LinkedIn is so powerful, of course) and, in particular, their peers.

25: Shades of Grey: What Authenticity Potential Really Means

Do you mould people into the version you think they should be or into the best possible versions of themselves?

Your answer instantly tells you what kind of leader you really are.

If it's the second, you are a true nurturer. If it's the first, you are undermining people's authenticity.

There is a lot of discussion today about the notion of authenticity. And yes, I concur with the likes of organisational psychologist Adam Grant and Stanford professor Jeffrey Pfeffer that we can't ever be 'fully' authentic. Turning up in our pyjamas to a meeting or saying exactly what we feel in every moment can certainly be career ending.

But I do think that a lot of people around the world – in almost every organisation – feel written off as individuals.

They feel they have to contort themselves into who they think they need to be, in order to be accepted at work (never mind to get ahead).

I have felt that myself while being led by others. And even despite that lived experience, I still often fell into the trap, as a CEO, of moulding people into what I thought I wanted to see.

It's been fascinating supporting the leadership team at JKS Restaurants, and I have been learning a lot with them about authenticity. It's core to what their guests experience and to how they operate as a team.

Anoothi Vishal, a restaurant critic, pointed out to me that it's only relatively recently that London restaurants were allowed to break out of the shackles of what they were expected to be.

JKS is a pioneer in this trend, and that's why I think London now has one of the best – perhaps the best – food scenes in the world.

As leaders, we deeply influence whether our people can be truly authentic or not.

But it's not an easy balance to achieve. To nurture authentic potential, we must focus on these key words: the best version of themselves they can possibly be.

Authenticity, in other words, has to be combined with excellence. If it isn't, it can easily become hollow – a lazy excuse for not holding ourselves to our highest standards.

Where leaders often go wrong is when they see concerns over underperformance. They jump to judgment and into corrective mode, panicking that they've given their teams too much leeway. Then they try to forcibly mould people in their own image to take back control. I certainly fell into that trap as a CEO.

The best nurturers insist on excellence, but they still see the other person as unique and allow them to behave differently. They can often see the person more deeply than they see themselves.

As Alice Sherwood points out in her recent book, Authenticity, true authenticity is more about shades of grey than black-and-white conceptions of what someone or something must be.

We can never be fully authentic.

Even the most authentic Iranian or Thai restaurant might serve a great British-brewed IPA. And that can add – rather than detract – from the dining experience.

When we decide what elements to change and adapt in this way – particularly to meet the requirements of excellence – then it becomes our choice. Not a choice imposed on us.

Perhaps the most important part of leadership today is to nurture others to change, evolve and grow, and to do so while allowing their authentic selves to shine through.

26: Prizing Open Windows: Revealing Our Hidden Selves

Ever heard of the Johari Window?

It explores what we can't see in ourselves but others can see (in other words, our blind spots); as well as what we do know about ourselves but want to hide from others because of embarrassment or even shame.

I think the best nurturers force us to smash through these panes of the Johari Window and fully understand all aspects of ourselves. And, in doing so, they unleash our potential.

There's always the temptation – at any stage of our careers or lives – for us to play the Mona Lisa: enigmatic, mysterious and not fully revealing anything of substance. It feels safer to remain unmoved by changing circumstances.

And the Mona Lisa smile is often how we're conditioned to think about leadership: that it's all about withstanding the shifting sands while keeping our 'mask' in place.

But at some point, as leaders, we need to stand for something. Something more constant and enduring. Something we deeply care about. Something we are willing to bet our reputations – perhaps even our careers – on. We need to reveal ourselves.

The best nurturers help us do that.

They don't force us to, but they create such a strong sense of emotional safety that it allows us to succumb to who we really are.

And they see us so clearly – often better than we see ourselves – that it feels futile to resist.

Whether it's how a tennis player hits their backhand or how a chef envisions their dishes, to do it truly authentically takes real courage. It takes courage to do things which align with who we are and what deeply drives us.

The best nurturers – whether it's a mentor, coach or manager – are able to suppress their own judgment when drawing out someone's true self. As I said in the last micro-chapter, they allow us to be the best version of ourselves and not who they think we should be.

That's why great nurturing is so hard and why great nurturers are so hard to come by.

Because they have to wear their own enigmatic smile to enable us to fully step out of our own shadow.

27: No Easy Answers: Asking the Right Questions at the Right Time

The best nurturers resist giving (easy) answers. Instead, they ask the right questions at the right time.

We talk a lot today about the importance of listening and sense-making as leadership attributes.

But the art of questioning is much less talked about – and much less understood – in nurturing potential. However, it's the critical step between listening and sense-making.

As leaders, we may have our own in-built hypothesis about an answer, but the best questions aren't rhetorical. They are built around genuine curiosity and care for the person we are nurturing.

But this requires suppressing our egos as nurturers. And (inevitably) that is hard. Especially when we have a lot of experience that we can bring to bear on tough questions.

Recently, I was supporting a CEO through a major inflection moment, and we were talking about the best organisational structure to navigate through it.

I felt so tempted to lurch towards possible solutions I had used during my own experience as a CEO. But I had to stop myself and remember that the CEO I was advising was a different person – with very different motivations and strengths – facing a different context and situation.

Here's the thing: it's not that my previous experience was irrelevant. In fact, it may have been deeply relevant. But I had to turn my easy answers into questions first.

For example, I asked what values were most important for the CEO to adhere to when devising the structure. And what success would feel like at the end of a restructure for her.

Listening carefully to her answers helped me to evaluate whether my own previous experience was relevant to the context. And whether to harness it to shape a solution or jettison it accordingly.

Irrespective of whether my potential solutions were relevant or not, I had walked in shoes similar to hers. And the empathy this engendered created a deep connection between us, allowing me to guide her with the most important questions.

So, questioning is not just the in-between step – it's the filter between listening and sense-making. Particularly in helping the people you are nurturing make sense, in their own unique way, of their realities (and you of yours).

There is a lot of talk these days about open questions. They can be powerful as they don't lead us to one answer or another. Often, however, they can be a somewhat lazy way to avoid identifying – and getting to the heart of – the issue at hand.

I prefer the idea of a 'pinpoint question': knowing the right question to ask at the right time based on our experience. The power of these questions comes in their timing and precision.

It's the question that helps someone both see a new perspective while also opening up to a potential new reality.

What pinpoint question will you ask someone today?

28: The How, Not the What: Originality versus Amplifying

Wanna be 'simply the best'? Then be an amplifier.

Focus more on the how and less on the what.

We lost an incredible voice and historical figure in Tina Turner this year. She was a trailblazer in music, history and civil rights.

As many insightful pieces on her life noted, Turner gained her initial success from amplifying the songs of others — including the Beatles and Led Zeppelin — well before she created original albums. It was the energy and verve with which she redelivered other people's songs that made them even more enduring and relevant.

Too often, I see people early in their careers becoming over-obsessed with two things:

The first is the cult of originality. The desire to produce something new and unique that will forever make your mark.

The second is a strong sense of what their careers should look like: what stage they should reach, in a specific career, at a predetermined point in time, that will signify 'success'.

But these stances are built on misconceptions. They're driven more by ego than by a desire for true excellence.

Originality is relative. Ultimately, there is nothing truly 'new' in this world. Creativity is often about how we repackage and repurpose existing work to make it more deeply relevant for the people we help and serve. As we develop confidence in what we are doing, we become ever more original in our own style. Hence, when Turner's first original album, Private Dancer, came out, she had already mastered many aspects of the rock and roll star performance. Her originality emerged organically after many years of growth and building on the work of others. It didn't pop into existence out of nowhere.

And how we 'show up' is usually much more important than what we actually do. What made Turner's first covers so successful is how 'all in' she was in her reinterpretation of the songs. She didn't let the fact it was someone else's material constrain her; she made them her own. She allowed the structure that was there to liberate her. And that enabled her to make the transition to creating her own songs. In the same way, we should worry less about what point we are at in our career and focus more on whether we are giving our best selves to our work in that moment.

Turner's life was — in my view — an affirmation: that creativity is a journey and not a fixed destination. And a celebration of the how in a world that is over-obsessed with the what.

As well as her belting tunes, she leaves behind a profound leadership legacy too.

29: What is Diversity? Finding Alignment

Diversity doesn't mean trying to be all things to all people.

We talk a lot today about diversity and inclusion, and these are critical pillars of any fair and just society. Not just in terms of gender, ethnicity or socioeconomic background, but also in terms of cognitive diversity and differences in working style. The evidence is also clear (across virtually all dimensions) that more diverse teams lead to better results.

But diverse hires still need to feel aligned with a common mission. One that is bigger than all of us. Without that alignment, our organisations will splinter.

One of my favourite insights from Jo Owen's wonderful book The Mindset of Success is this: leaders hire for skills, but they fire for values.

Too often, when we are selecting people for a role, we only want to hire 'the best'.

There's a certain reductive logic in that, of course. But it belies the fact that defining 'the best' is itself highly subjective.

I teach at the University of Cambridge. Talking to undergraduate admissions leaders there, the Cambridge supervision is best suited to a particular type of student. One who enjoys the practice of regular small group discussions and constructive challenge, often under deadline pressure.

A university like Cambridge is, of course, world-leading, but it's not perfectly suited to everyone (no matter how intellectually bright they may be).

We are better off being really clear what we – our organisations and ourselves as leaders – truly stand for. We need to articulate what our purpose and perspective is, what the inflection moments ahead look like for us and what we are looking for in others to collectively reach it.

I was impressed by a collection of ads I saw on the London Underground as I recently walked out of Oval station. They were beautifully micro-targeted towards the many Indian cricket fans attending the World Test Championship nearby.

I think this micro-targeting principle applies to how we should hire too. We need to reach for the specific people that deeply share the values, purpose and passion of the organisation or team we lead.

And once we've found these people, who are hopefully diverse in every other way, their potential can't be left to chance; it has to be nurtured actively, especially if they come from underrepresented backgrounds of any type.

If you're an employee, it's important to express your own sense of personal mission – what kind of work you really want to do, how you want to do it and the kind of working culture you really want to do it in.

Increasingly, I see the world of careers and work as a 'marriage' between employers and employees – each achieving each other's missions.

But it feels like a lot of organisations today are still taking far too many accidental prisoners. Capturing people under false pretences with generic hiring practices and then slowly realising (or not) that there's a huge mismatch on both sides. We've seen the results of this in the recent and growing trend of 'quiet quitting'.

So, diversity doesn't mean being all things to all people.

Diversity means attracting and deeply aligning very different people to achieve a common and truly purposeful thing.

30: Opportunity Hoarding: Opening Up Our Networks to Pay It Forward

Can you be a fantastic networker and an 'opportunity hoarder' at the same time? Sadly, yes.

All of us who are leaders have made it somewhere near the top of our organisations. Most know that we owe that success to social capital: to our relationships with leaders above us who opened up our ambitions and thinking, created new pathways, built opportunities for special projects and unblocked career impediments.

But we can easily forget this once we reach the summit of the mountain. It's more comforting to believe we got there because of our own talent. At these moments, we tend to focus on the blood, sweat and tears of our journey.

But the truth is that it was because someone else believed in – and then tangibly backed – our potential.

Without that backing, innate talent – no matter how strong – will never convert into forward- looking potential.

So, what's the easiest way for us as leaders to pay our success forward?

I think it's to open up our address books. It's easy to feel guarded when we are asked to introduce someone. What happens if the introduction doesn't go well? Or what if they meet and say bad things about us? Those anxieties – along with a misguided belief that we are the ones responsible for our own success – can lead us to become opportunity hoarders. Keeping our resources to ourselves because we think that's how we will hold on to our power.

Opening up networks can indeed make us deeply insecure.

But it's something I believe we fundamentally need to do as leaders in order to nurture potential.

And the wonderful thing about starting with that is this – networks are subject to network effects. Rather than being finite – if I introduce you to someone, I can't introduce someone else – network capital is infinite and self-reinforcing. That connection you spark will undoubtedly lead to further connections being made from there.

Don't worry about asking each person for a reciprocal introduction. It will happen naturally at the right time.

And trust me, as the person making the introduction, your standing will grow.

There are lots of ways to nurture another person's potential, but opening up our networks is the most powerful way to start.

31: Run Towards Generosity: Building Networks Founded on Trust, Letting Go and Intentionality

A great network is critical to our success.

It's not just about giving those below you the leg up to pay it forward. Relationships and social capital are critical to our careers – especially as we advance towards leadership positions.

But as I said in the previous micro-chapter, we often hold back. Niggling worries stop us from taking the leap and making introductions. What if something goes wrong after I put these two people in touch?

Here's the travesty: for every introduction made, there are 10 that could have been.

Ten that could have made a meaningful difference to someone's life and career (and I have been the beneficiary of many, especially at my own career inflections).

Ironically, it's this inclination to hold back that stymies our own network and our own success. The answer is to run in the exact opposite direction.

Towards generosity.

Generosity in making connections requires an important trio: trust, letting go and intentionality.

Trust doesn't mean believing the person you are introducing is perfect. (If that was the bar, I would never have been introduced to many of the people I now get to work with and learn from.) It means you trust in their sincerity and integrity. If you have a basic level of trust in these two areas, make the introduction.

Letting go is not feeling responsible for the outcome of that introduction (a principle I learned from my friend and networking great Vikas Pota). Both people you are connecting are grown-ups, and they know you aren't to blame for how they interact as individuals. The chemistry may or may not match. Irrespective, they will appreciate you making the effort to introduce them.

Letting go is also about not expecting 'payback'. We have all come across the 'I'll scratch your back, you scratch mine' mentality that can give the whole concept of networking such a shallow and transactional feeling. Don't worry about payback; whether indirectly or directly, generosity almost always gets rewarded over the medium- and long-term. (If you want the psychological evidence behind this phenomenon, read Adam Grant's Give and Take).

Then there's the final principle: be intentional. Look proactively for opportunities to make useful connections. And then put a small amount of effort into this every day. One introduction a day will take five minutes of your time – and I can promise you there will be few better uses of it. Personally, I try to make introductions first thing in the morning so they don't get crowded out by other commitments.

I wanted to 'walk my own talk' when it came to living these principles, so I set up the Intrinsic Leadership Network. I feel fortunate and privileged to deeply support an amazing group of leaders across sectors and countries. This enables those leaders to meet, learn and connect with each other to better share their expertise.

If we can learn to embrace generosity in this area of our lives, we'll soon receive it.

32: Access All Areas: Being in The Room Where It Happens

Are you in The Room Where It Happens? And do you let others into the room?

My two sons fell in love with the musical Hamilton over the lockdown. And the message of that story – that a country's fate was sealed at a single dinner, in a single room, on a single night – has stayed with me.

This year I had the privilege of facilitating the JKS Restaurants leadership team retreat. JKS is at such an exciting inflection moment in its growth. It was fascinating to help steer the discussion in The Room Where It Happens.

As a leader, if you are serious about nurturing your own potential, you must of course make sure you are in the right room, at the right time, to contribute to the most important decisions.

However, equally importantly, make sure the room is open to others – in two ways.

We can talk to exhaustion about creating environments where everyone achieves their full potential, in work and life. But it's all just empty words, mood music, if we don't take action towards that.

First, give your team opportunities to be in the room with you and your most senior colleagues. Think out loud with them, even if it's initially uncomfortable. Be open, vulnerable and share your hopes and fears. Be honest about risks and trade-offs. Help frame the broader context to enable them to make the best decisions.

Second, make sure the people you're nurturing have access to the more private you. Use a confidential room where you can check in with them beyond the day-to-day tasks and help them to unblock impediments in an honest and open environment. While many organisations run employee surveys, my client Brian Sims conducts regular one-to-one check-ins with his team based around the 12 Gallup questions. For example, one of these is: do I have the opportunity to do my best every day? The feedback and conversation that springs from this is as important as the question.

This is one of our most important roles as leaders – not only to be in the right rooms but to pry open the doors for others.

The doors that lead us to where the most memorable tunes – individually and collectively – are really composed.

33: Helping Those in the Ring: We Must Nurture Potential as Leaders

Our people fight in the ring every day to bring our mission into being. In the ring, life is tough.

If we're fortunate to stand outside the ring, as leaders, our role is clear: to deeply nurture those who box within it on our behalf.

We can't just be spectators or armchair critics. We have to be their second eyes. The second eyes of the tiger.

To do this, we need to nurture them. Nurturing is not the same as traditional managing, coaching or mentoring – the normal methods we think of when supporting others to fulfil their true potential.

Coaching (at least in its purest forms) is open-ended – based on the assumption that the person you are nurturing knows best. That can be true, but often – especially at inflection moments – there are a lot of different thoughts and ideas fighting for space in someone's mind, much of it conflicting. A great nurturer can help provide constructive challenge and exposure to different perspectives to help draw out their true direction and potential.

On the other hand, mentoring can be too leading and even prescriptive. The fact that 'I did it this way and it worked' only has limited validity. Even if it's comparing two very similar situations, it's the struggle and the journey – the sense that an individual has tussled with the various options and found a way through – that really matters.

I see nurturing, then, as the space between coaching and mentoring.

Nurturing is all about unlocking authenticity, connection and excellence (ACE) within each person in the ring. Individually and as a collective group.

ACE is like a three-legged stool: all three legs need to be in place to feel balanced.

Authenticity is about helping the person in the ring be the best version of themselves. Connection is about helping them feel motivated by their work and the people they are ultimately serving. Excellence is about having tough, critical conversations when needed – but always out of concern for the mission and the person's best interests.

So, please reflect and ask yourself this question: how can I help those in the ring unlock their authenticity, connection and excellence? How can I help them nurture their own true potential?

Reflective Questions from Section 3: Ignite Potential in Ourselves and Others

1. To what extent do the people you lead understand your perspective, what really matters to you and what you stand for? What can you do to make this clearer for them?

2. How much do you rely on screening talent versus nurturing potential more deeply when it comes to the people you lead? What could help you be a more intentional nurturer?

3. Is the culture of your team or organisation more 'hardball' or 'softball'? If the former, how can you move it towards being more 'soft hardball' as a minimum?

4. When it comes to your own potential, what ways are there to realise your goals directly? What are the stepping stones to get there?

5. What privilege baggage are you still holding onto? How can you lighten that load so you can really focus on what matters to you?

6. How can you combine authenticity with connection and excellence in the people you are nurturing?

7. In what ways could you improve your listening skills, to really help the people you are nurturing feel comfortable sharing their hidden selves?

8. How can you let more of the people you lead into The Rooms Where It Happens?

9. What are the three things you could do to open up your networks for others?

DIAL FRAMEWORK RECAP:

Dare a new direction (the hour hand)

Ignite potential in ourselves and others (the minute hand)

Align motivations (the second hand)

Learn to learn (the watch dial)

SECTION 4:

THE SECOND HAND:
ALIGN MOTIVATIONS

---

*I*n Section 3, we examined how we can create organisations and societies where our individual and collective potential can be nurtured.

In Section 4, we'll move our focus to staying motivated and resilient as we navigate our key inflection moments, both for ourselves and those we lead – particularly through harnessing internal (intrinsic) motivation. We'll look at two forms of purpose – big 'P' purpose and small 'p' purpose – and the importance of the latter in particular (helping and serving others, each and every day) in driving and sustaining our daily motivation. We'll also look at the tool of personal mission statements and how we can more intentionally allocate our time towards what fundamentally drives us. We'll explore the critical difference between autonomy and flexibility and how to have sensitive but constructive discussions with colleagues and stakeholders on how to achieve both. We'll examine the critical role of mastery as a motivator and how we can achieve it in the broadest possible sense, harnessing inflection moments to achieve regular progress towards our goals. Finally, we'll debunk traditional myths around career choices (e.g. generalist versus specialist) and consider how to harness motivation to create really distinct career positioning. (For those interested in going even deeper in this area, please read my first book, Intrinsic.)

In this part of the book, we'll cover the following micro-chapters:

- It's the Journey: Intrinsic and Extrinsic Motivation
- A Million Lives: Finding Motivation in Our Small 'p' Purpose
- Our Productivity Crisis: Aligning with Our Small 'p' Purpose
- Guided Autonomy: Setting Our Autonomy Guardrails as Leaders
- Human Skills: How Mastery Arms Us for Inflection Moments
- Bringing Out the Human: Fostering Motivation Through Shared Humanity
- Mastery Isn't Selfish: It's About Enhancing a Whole Field (Not Just Ourselves)

- Being at the Wheel: The Danger of Confusing Flexibility and Autonomy
- An Artificial Choice: Generalist versus Specialist Career Paths
- Our Category of One: Positioning Ourselves and Our Unique Purpose

34. It's the Journey: Intrinsic and Extrinsic Motivation

What gives us peace as leaders?

Recently, I had the honour of receiving my OBE at Windsor Castle, from HRH Princess Anne. We had many things to talk about, from our shared passion for education and young people, to our experiences in Uganda (from where she had just returned).

That special day – which I was able to share with my wife, Aida, and with my parents – made me reflect on the nature of leadership success today.

I had the most amazing decade founding and leading education NGO STiR Education. It's gone from strength to strength, impacting millions more children, since I handed it over two years ago to Girish Menon, Jo Owen and their amazing team.

Looking back now, those 10 years were the most exhilarating – and challenging – of my life.

It wasn't easy. As a father of two young boys, I basically lived on a plane. We suffered daily setbacks, from challenges in working with emerging country governments, to the near constant pressures of fundraising, to seeing deeply loved colleagues pass away.

I was a highly imperfect leader. With the benefit of hindsight, I'm conscious that I could have done so many things better. And I'm conscious that many others – including those in my team – were just as deserving of this award as me.

But when I stepped into Windsor Castle, I felt a strange sense of calm and peace.

A sense that however imperfect a leader I'd been, I'd given it everything. Every dream, every sinew, every ounce of energy I had.

As leaders, that's all that we can ultimately do. We can't control the outcome. We can only do our best to set a direction that we believe is authentic and right. And to deeply inspire others to travel with us while we nurture their potential.

Our sense of accomplishment as leaders comes from that fundamental truth: leadership is messy. There are few predetermined answers, let alone 'right' answers. And no matter how hard you work, or how 'successful' you are, there is always more – especially with hindsight – you could have done.

It requires us to acknowledge that we will never be perfect.

What matters most is that we throw everything at it, stay humble and learn, and most of all enjoy the ride.

That was the irony of the whole day for me. The OBE was, in many ways, the most extrinsic (external) of motivators. And yet it meant so much. But I could never have sustained shedding the blood, sweat and tears required to lead the organisation if the intrinsic (inner) drive wasn't there. The journey had to be worth it for its own sake – it had to have its own sense of purpose, autonomy and mastery (the drivers of intrinsic motivation that we'll explore in this section).

In fact, it was the intrinsic motivation – and the very fact that I'd been able to stay in the proverbial ring leading the organisation for a decade – that made the extrinsic motivation feel real and tangible. It is what gave the OBE meaning.

Although we'll focus this section mostly on intrinsic motivators (because these are what we have generally ignored as leaders), we need both forms of motivation in our lives – and they complement and even reinforce each other.

It's wonderful to now help other leaders – across so many diverse sectors – revel in that ride. Because that day in Windsor Castle was a moving reminder of how incredible the ride had been for me.

35: A Million Lives: Finding Motivation in Our Small 'p' Purpose

100,000,000 lives.

100 leaders.

Which matters more?

Over the last two and a half years, I've been able to support more than 100 leaders, across numerous sectors and countries, as they face major inflection moments in their organisations and leadership journeys.

I recently did a quick back-of-the-envelope calculation.

Collectively, these 100 leaders impact more than 100 million lives through their work (and that's a conservative estimate!)

I used to get seduced by these big numbers – or what I call big 'P' purpose. I think of our big 'P' purpose as how we contribute to a much bigger wicked problem, where there is no easy, technical answer. And I would define leadership at inflection moments as a fundamentally wicked problem.

But as sexy as the 100 million number sounds, the truth is that it's not my impact. In other words, I didn't directly engage with or even know these people.

My direct impact is on the 100 leaders: my role has to be to empower them to reach places they wouldn't have reached otherwise.

I call this our small 'p' purpose – being motivated by and grounded in our work by the people we directly help and serve.

Big 'P' purpose is useful as it provides us with a 'North Star' – a point to aim for to ensure that we are spending our time addressing a problem that is important and deeply meaningful to us. But that's all it is. The risk of letting it take over is that we can get lost in the grand illusions created by big numbers and lose focus on those we make a difference to directly, each day, every day.

When I look back at my experience leading STiR, it's not the millions of children that the work impacted that I see as my most important leadership legacy. It's the 200 or so staff who were involved in the organisation at various points to whom I made a direct difference. When I see them awarded prestigious scholarships as 'alumni' or take on leadership roles in government or the non-profit sector, that's when I feel most fulfilled.

Similarly, you can be a CEO of a 20,000-strong organisation with millions of customers and see your impact that way. Or you can look at your 10-person leadership team and realise that's where you have the most to contribute each day – helping them to reach places they wouldn't have reached without you.

Think of it as the law of proximate impact. Focus on the people you actually help and serve. Our small 'p' purpose is what keeps us motivated each day, every day.

I have to trust that if I do my best to nurture the potential of great leaders, they will go on to impact hundreds of millions of lives.

There's their impact, and there's mine – and they need to be clearly distinguished.

36: Our Productivity Crisis: Aligning with Our Small 'p' Purpose

What's causing our productivity crisis?

Think-tanks like The Brookings Institution have elaborated some powerful hypotheses for the reasons why productivity in developed countries has been falling off a cliff. That's a phenomenon that's well documented, from the speeches of national leaders to the press.

But I think there's a deeper culprit at play.

What's really going on is a full-blown purpose and motivation crisis. And it's a crisis of two parts:

1. The inability of most people in our workforce to define their motivation and purpose in the first place.

2. The inability of the same people to spend their time on what motivates them most deeply (and where they can have a substantial impact).

But why is this happening to us now?

We no longer live in societies where the majority of us produce widgets (or the equivalent) on an assembly line. Most developed economies are dominated by service industries.

'Productivity' is therefore a challenging concept to measure in the first place.

As an example, I was standing in an airport immigration queue recently watching an immigration officer spend an hour with a passenger to resolve what looked like a serious visa issue. By modern metrics, processing just one passenger was 'low productivity'. But her intervention almost certainly made a life- changing difference to the person concerned. She was fulfilling her small 'p' purpose.

For this reason, I just don't think job descriptions (at least in their current form) really work anymore. They're too cookie-cutter and formulaic.

I prefer the idea of a personal mission statement that describes your goals – your small 'p' purpose. And the phrases 'I help … to … by …' can provide the scaffolding for this statement – the description of how you'll reach those goals.

Describing our small 'p' purpose can often feel mundane when it's seemingly the most obvious things to which we need to anchor our motivation and time. But you'd be surprised how easily we can drift away from them. That's why a personal mission statement can be so powerful.

Mine is the following:

'I help leaders and organisations to navigate inflection moments and futureproof their success by advising, facilitating and writing.'

I find having a personal mission statement helps me to align my time much better as I focus my activities on these goals.

I also find that if I'm spending at least half of my time fulfilling my personal mission statement, I become much more motivated. And if I can spend more than two thirds of my time on it, I'm in a really good place – both in terms of motivation and impact.

There are three great strategies you can employ to spend more time on the activities in your personal mission statement:

- **Eliminating and automating:** Do you need to do that thing yourself? For example, I used to spend hours scheduling things (as I preferred not to have a PA). Now I use Calendly as a simple way to move things around – and it's saved hours of my week.

- **Delegating:** Can I pass the activity on to others? As a CEO, I found myself attending many meetings where someone else in my team could have attended just as ably – and it would have been a good way for me to help nurture their potential.

- **Reframing:** Can I do the thing but achieve deeper small 'p' purpose from it? For example, given that I work across different countries, I have a lot of my meetings with CEOs online. When I meet in person (when they're in London, for instance), I therefore want to explore how they are doing much more deeply – and at a personal level – and to celebrate what they have achieved. That face-to-face interaction shouldn't just be like every other meeting.

This is where I think AI can be so powerful as a 'co-pilot'. It enables us to do more of the above and takes away so much of the mundanity of how we currently spend our time. This really hit me while working with primary care leaders across the UK's NHS.

Being productive today is no longer about working more hours or doing more in a fixed amount of time. We can easily be busy in this way, with never-ending meetings and emails (so busy that we don't even have time for the bathroom). But we won't necessarily achieve my definition of leadership unless we focus that time on our end goal – to really enable others to reach places they wouldn't have reached otherwise.

We can find a way out of our current productivity crisis, but only if we re-diagnose the problem in the first place.

We need to see it as a motivation and purpose crisis.

37: Guided Autonomy: Setting Our Autonomy Guardrails as Leaders

We need to talk about autonomy.

As I said in Section 3, I increasingly see work as a 'marriage'. We work as leaders to achieve an organisation's mission. But the organisation is also there to help us achieve our personal mission statement.

If this marriage is to last, both sides need to achieve the level of autonomy that is 'just right' for them.

Because for each of us, as unique individuals, there is a different definition of 'just right'. And for each organisation, there is an equivalent 'just right' based on the work it seeks to do.

Leaders thus need to set their autonomy guardrails clearly based on where these 'just right' areas converge.

If they don't, we end up with un unworkable imbalance: either complete anarchy where each of us ends up as a 'lone ranger' at one extreme, or a strong sense of feeling stifled and micro-managed at the other.

I see these dynamics play out a lot in the UK parliament, where I have been doing some research. Some MPs and peers see themselves as 'lone rangers'; other MPs are criticised by the press as 'poodles' to their parties.

But what does 'just right' mean when it comes to being a political leader? It's such an important role in our society, and yet we haven't really developed a common perspective.

Leaders can find their 'just right' zone if they stop and reflect on a few questions:

- What does the organisation truly stand for?
- What does it want to ensure happens consistently for the customer/community/citizen they are helping and serving?
- And what are the true 'non-negotiables' in that?

If the answers to these questions are clear, that can provide the direction and alignment that everyone needs.

It provides the guardrails for our autonomy.

And that way, no one falls off the cart as we hurtle down our leadership road.

38: Human Skills: How Mastery Arms Us for Inflection Moments

Mastery matters. It's the ace up our sleeves as leaders at an inflection moment. But what does it really mean?

It's not about an end goal. We may never reach the top of the mountain; we may never reach nirvana. Even a tennis great like Roger Federer feels they have never played the perfect tenWs set. It's the journey, not the destination.

And mastery is not about comparison or competition. When we play the perfect set in our minds, it's not against a Nadal or a Djokovic. It's against ourselves.

In my first book, Intrinsic, I defined mastery as the journey to become the best version of ourselves we can be.

And that's what makes mastery so deeply motivating. We can always keep improving; we can always grow. Seeing progress motivates us to put more effort in, which in turn leads to more progress – and that can create a virtuous cycle between mastery and our (intrinsic) motivation.

I also wrote about how mastery is quickly migrating away from technical skills towards more human ones as the former become automated. In the last couple of years, the AI boom has massively accelerated the speed of that change.

Career expert Jonathan Winter – who chairs the Careers Innovation Company – shared some fascinating insights with me about where mastery may be going. He cited the increasingly important role of judgment, particularly judgment around context, which is something that we as humans are still best placed to provide. He also spoke about new areas of mastery, such as the ability to make connections across domains and to frame everything we do around purpose.

At inflection moments, we often underestimate the mastery we have accumulated over our careers – particularly these more human dimensions that we have built over years (and thousands of hours) of experience. They tend not to be on our job description and so we discount these skills and the potential they give us. And that's one of the reasons we tend to play it safe in make-or-break moments.

There's a wonderful word that I recently encountered in discussion with senior leaders at the education organisation Teach For All – elasticity. The elasticity to move in a different direction, take a risk, do the unexpected. These human skills that we have mastered empower us to do this if we'd only recognise and acknowledge them. It's like the proverbial joker in our pack of cards

The truth is that we all have our jokers. The necessity of inflection moments means that we should feel able to play them when we need to.

39: Bringing Out the Human: Fostering Motivation Through Shared Humanity

The concept of fostering more human leadership and workplaces has grown in popularity in recent years and for very good reason. It's not only the right thing to do; it's been demonstrated to attract people to organisations and keep them fulfilled and motivated in their work in the long-term.

And there's another benefit. Mastery of the most human of skills will allow you to thrive as a leader, and it will speak to your intrinsic motivation as well as your teams.

So, how should we 'show up' as leaders to ensure we and our organisations are truly human?

1. Build a leadership style that achieves the desired outcomes but still respects our people's autonomy and those of their teams. We can do this by listening deeply to our team members (at all levels), but also by taking tough and unpopular decisions when needed.

2. Trust our people's fundamental judgment as professionals (with some basic safeguards, of course).

3. Understand the different motivational archetypes of our teams and personalise our approaches accordingly.

4. Balance the needs of individuals with the common good of the team – and sacrifice our own personal interests when necessary.

5. See talent and potential in all our team members, and provide them with paths to grow within our organisation and beyond.

6. Allow our team members to take intentional risks to enable them to learn and grow from the feedback.

7. Share and reveal more about ourselves as people – including our vulnerabilities – to encourage our team members to do the same.

8. Reflect deeply on the core nature of the work we are collectively undertaking – and how we can work together as a team to organise it as humanly as possible.

In short, as leaders, we need to:

- see work as more human;
- be more human; and
- be humanity role models to our teams.

Too often, as leaders, we have gotten seduced by paint-by-numbers approaches to leadership. We have created inflexible, one-size-fits-all structures, targets and compliance that encourage our teams not to think much. Or think at all.

The paradox is that, in the short term, results can sometimes improve. But they are rarely sustained. And what we create, in denying the humanity of our teams, is an enormous recruitment and retention crisis – something which will haunt future generations.

By creating a rock-solid foundation that will speak to people's intrinsic motivation and your own, you'll be able to seize the promise in your team and in your own leadership.

40: Mastery Isn't Selfish: It's About Enhancing a Whole Field (Not Just Ourselves)

What makes a 'great' truly great?

I think it goes beyond being just a great individual performer (important as that is).

I think true greats evolve and grow their role. They eventually become ambassadors and even custodians of their field.

They don't just lift their own mastery and performance. They lift their whole field – and others in that field – along with them.

As I share in my book Intrinsic, tennis is a highly individual sport, and it's therefore particularly susceptible to what I call 'winner takes all' dynamics. For example:

1. The tennis Holy Trinity – Nadal, Federer, Djokovic – have scooped more than 60 grand slam titles between them.

2. Federer has become tennis's first ever billionaire.

Yet I would argue that their dominance has also led to a better outcome for all top professionals. For instance:

1. Overall prize money at Wimbledon has almost tripled over the last 15 years.

2. Prize money has increased almost five-fold for those losing in the early rounds over the same period.

3. There's now a pension scheme for players and a much better 'cushion' for all players (in terms of well-being, rest time and travel, for example).

And the proof is in the pudding: seeing the explosion of younger, high-potential players at Wimbledon this year – including Brandon Nakashima – was such a treat.

Greats don't just succeed in a field. They learn to make the whole field brighter and richer, just as these stars make Centre Court – the home of tennis – even more magical when they step foot on the grass. Even if it means drawing in talent who will eventually challenge them.

Players like Federer and Nadal were naturals at making that leap to ambassador for their sport, and they take their positions of power and influence seriously, but it often isn't easy to transition from being a great performer to a great custodian. We need to think about this mastery transition intentionally and make sure that we embrace it at the right time.

For those interested in these questions of intrinsic motivation and potential, my previous book, Intrinsic, goes much deeper into these areas.

And if you want to know more about how this happened in practice in the world of tennis, listen to 'Embracing Each Moment Like Roger Federer', an enlightening episode of Simon Mundie's podcast, Life Lessons.

Can you think of greats in other fields who evolved their role in a similar way? Please let me know!

41: Being at the Wheel: The Danger of Confusing Flexibility and Autonomy

Why are workers losing the flexible-working battle?

A recent piece on Grindr in the Los Angeles Times made me sit up and listen. (Just in case you are wondering: no, I have never used the app!) The company lost half its workforce when it instituted a strict two-day a week return to the physical office.

It seems as if this battle is going on across many different organisations right now, particularly after the paradigm-changing COVID-19 pandemic. I think the reason that employers and employees are at loggerheads is that they are both fighting a different battle. (I realise that as leaders we usually wear the dual hat of employer and employee, but I'm going to assume our main hat is as an employer here.)

As employers, we can often see this as a flexibility issue – something that benefits only our employees rather than our wider organisation.

But it's really an autonomy issue – something that affects employers and employees and which, if we can reframe the problem, can be resolved to benefit both.

The truth is that our employees have lost fundamental autonomy over their most precious resource – their time. When being forced to go back to the office, many of them dread the inevitable time drain of commuting, meetings and unnecessary office distractions.

I define autonomy at work as feeling at the wheel of our work lives. There is huge evidence (that I shared in my first book, Intrinsic) around the positive effect of autonomy on productivity and motivation.

Far too much of work today is synchronous when it be could be asynchronous.

Far too much of our time is spent on catch-ups and meetings that don't pass three basic autonomy tests; questions that each of our employees should ask themselves:

1. **Difference:** If I hadn't been here, would anything have changed in impact and outcome?

2. **Delegation:** Could someone in my team have done just as good a job as me?

3. **Development:** Did this help me develop or learn about my role more broadly and/or learn about my organisation?

If the answer to all three questions is no, your employees should be able to achieve the same outcome asynchronously.

So, as we return to work and the office, a suggestion: Support your employees to not just ask for greater flexibility. Support them to ask for greater autonomy.

42: An Artificial Choice: Generalist versus Specialist Career Paths

Should we be aiming to be generalists or specialists?

There's been a real desire to jump on one of these bandwagons. (David Epstein's great book Range is an impassioned case for the value of generalists, for example.)

However, I think both views are misguided when it comes to how we think about mastery.

I think mastery today is about being able to flexibly adopt different combinations of each based on our career stage and our precise role.

In my case, my 'mastery map' has had an hourglass shape. I started as a generalist in consulting and then spent 15 years going deep into the world of education, particularly focusing on the role of teaching. Now I am back to a more generalist profile as I advise leaders across sectors.

Many younger leaders I speak to are concerned about 'going deep'. They worry that the specialist expertise they gain around a technical domain won't transfer.

But this worry about getting 'too narrow' in our careers can be misguided. I think what's important to stress is that it's the broader essential skills that we need to develop and master, irrespective of how specialist or generalist we become.

Essentials like influence, communication, advocacy and nurturing potential, to name but a few.

These are the fundamental human skills that will make the biggest difference to our success as a leader.

These essentials can be gained whether what we do is more specialist or generalist. And they can help us transfer across sectors or even countries.

Moreover, by going deep into an area, we can really make a unique point of difference and contribution between ourselves and others – we can stretch ourselves to our limits. And it's this stretching of ourselves that will develop these broader essentials most effectively. Indeed, the deeper we go into a technical area, the deeper the opportunities are to do this.

Let's acknowledge that neither generalist nor specialist is a 'better' career path. It's about what deeply motivates us in the moment, and where we can make the biggest difference in the world. And the decision as to which path to pursue will vary over time.

Instead, let's focus on acquiring those broader mastery essentials. Would you agree?

43: Our Category of One: Positioning Ourselves and Our Unique Purpose

Have you found your career 'category of one'?

I love this term from my friend Utkarsh Amitabh, the founder of Network Capital.

In other words, have you found a clear, distinct and authentic career niche that you can uniquely occupy? Categories of one are a great goal to reach.

But how do you decide which category of one to focus on? It's not always an easy journey.

My own personal career change is revealing on this topic. Three years ago – after writing Intrinsic – I sought to become the go-to person on intrinsic motivation and leadership. I was excited to have found my purpose.

However, when I actually started working with amazing leaders, I realised I was getting into much broader terrain. At the core, I seemed to be helping leaders and their teams with their key inflection moments: helping them futureproof their success and shape what the next chapter of their organisations would look like.

I started with what I thought was a clear sense of my big 'P' purpose – a wider problem that I wanted to contribute to.

But I needed to ground myself in what the people I was actually helping and serving (i.e. leaders) actually needed from me – my small 'p' purpose.

And I love my focus on inflection moments because I get to have a much broader lens to support the leaders I work with.

Career positioning is an evolving journey. Being intentional is critical, but so is having the humility to deeply listen to those we help and serve. That's how we can balance our big 'P' contribution with our tangible small 'p' impact.

Choosing a category of one is critical.

But we need to realise that category may evolve over time – and that's a good thing.

Over our careers, we can be working towards creating a category of one; while, on our journey, we voyage through categories of many.

Happy voyaging – because it's the journey of discovery itself that is the most motivating.

Reflective Questions from Section 4: Align Motivations

1. *How do the concepts of big 'P' and small 'p' purpose apply to you and your own life as a leader?*

2. *Please write down your personal mission statement by using the scaffolding structure of 'I help … to … by …', (My example would be: I help leaders across sectors to navigate inflection points and futureproof success by advising, facilitating and writing).*

3. *How will you put as much time as possible into your personal mission statement activities? What do you need to do to (i) eliminate, (ii) delegate and (iii) reframe your purpose in order to achieve that?*

4. *What does autonomy with guardrails – or guided autonomy – look like for you in your role? How can you have a conversation with those around you about how they can achieve both more autonomy and more flexibility (realising that they are separate concepts)?*

5. *What are the broader essentials of mastery you need to have in your current role? Alternatively, what new areas of mastery do you want to develop in your new role? How can you do this regardless of whether you are evolving towards a generalist or a specialist career track?*

6. *How can you get closer to discovering your category of one, and what is that category likely to be?*

DIAL FRAMEWORK RECAP:

Dare a new direction (the hour hand)

Ignite potential in ourselves and others (the minute hand)

Align motivations (the second hand)

Learn to learn (the watch dial)

SECTION 5:

THE WATCH DIAL:
LEARN TO LEARN

---

*I*n Section 4, we explored the critical role of staying motivated and resilient through our inflection moments. One of the key areas we explored was mastery – becoming the best versions of ourselves we can be.

In Section 5, our focus moves on to learning new skills, developing new areas of expertise and (where needed) even reinventing ourselves; it's about learning to learn. In this section, we'll look at how to build the right learning-to-learn 'muscle' and orient ourselves towards becoming a true lifelong learner through new mindsets and day-to-day habits. We'll look at everything from how to change careers to how to keep our leadership perspective updated and fresh. We'll consider how taking a lifelong learning perspective may end up challenging conventional views of success. We'll learn to recognise others for their learning progress, how to forgive, and how to intentionally develop new areas of learning.

In this part of the book, we'll cover the following micro-chapters:

- Your Education Is Only the Beginning: The Critical Importance of Lifelong Learning
- Embrace Being a Beginner: How to Keep Learning Something New
- Walk the Tightrope: Committing to Career Change
- Jumping off the Treadmill: How to Keep Your Learning Perspective Fresh
- Should I Stay or Should I Go? Deciding When to Leave a Role
- Calming the Fire: Emotional Intelligence and Learning to Forgive
- Twists and Turns: Trusting the Value of the Crooked Learning Journey
- Celebrate the Leap: Valuing Action over Inaction at Inflection Moments
- Vanquishing Impostor Syndrome: Learning How to Leap into Leadership
- The Beauty of Sunsets: The Courage to Reinvent Ourselves

44: Your Education Is Only the Beginning: The Critical Importance of Lifelong Learning

Will a fancy degree make you an emperor? Or will it be like the emperor's new clothes?

I think the answer (thankfully) is neither. And that was reaffirmed by my wonderful INSEAD 20-year alumni reunion this year where we had the chance to visit the shimmering, refurbished Château de Fontainebleau. The rich, honest conversations I had with my former classmates and faculty clarified something for me. True learning is different from education. Our degrees were only the very beginning.

Here's what I thought would happen on graduation day, two decades ago – and what real life offered instead:

1. I thought my career and life would be a beautiful, upward straight line towards success.

Instead, life was a series of zig-zags. There were many bumps, setbacks and frustrations amidst the successes. The key was not to get disheartened, to keep motivated and stay the course.

2. I thought I could do it alone.

Instead, it was the conversations with my classmates and friends – often at the most difficult junctures – that gave me the confidence and perspective to overcome problems and harness opportunities.

3. I thought there were clear 'rules' of success.

Instead, I realised that everyone – including our so-called leaders – was making it up as they went along. So, I had to discover my own rules, as thoughtfully as I could.

4. I thought others would lead us.

Instead, I learned that if we don't lead ourselves, no one else will. There are so many things, big and small, that we need to do to create a better world, and we can't assume they will be taken care of by others. We need to start from within.

5. I thought it was about making it to the destination – the proverbial château.

Instead, I found the journey – with all its twists and turns – was far more interesting. It was the sense of being alive and living a life of meaning (in whatever way matters to us) that meant so much more. It was about getting lost in something bigger than ourselves and trying to make a difference to others.

In short, a fancy degree – whether at INSEAD or anywhere else – is just the first step in your learning journey. It's all about opening us up to others and the world around us so that we can continue to grow and evolve. That's what makes it such a life (and perspective) changing experience.

These experiences and the new perspectives they offer us can help to prepare us more fully – individually and collectively – for the adventures and lessons that life can bring.

With gratitude to all those who have been on that adventure with me.

45: Embrace Being a Beginner: How to Keep Learning Something New

We're all going to need to be lifelong learners, if you believe anyone from McKinsey & Company to Yuval Noah Harari.

There's hope. We can all learn to learn – as a recent experience showed me.

I retried yoga. My motivation was simple: to restore much needed flexibility to my knees. They've been taking a pounding from the tennis I play four or five times a week.

The first time I'd tried yoga was at an outdoor sunset session in Bali 11 years ago. It was a stunning setting. But I was intimidated by the effortless flow of the yogis around me. And yes, by them often looking down their noses at me. I'd never tried it since.

This time, I was lucky to have the amazing Lina Crossley as an instructor. And I came out loving it – and not just for my knees' sake.

So, what's the best way to keep learning something new? Here are six key things I learned:

1. Reserve judgment and resist comparison.

When you start something new, don't obsess about being objectively 'good'.

I found myself glancing at the other yogis in the room to see how I compared. I found out that was futile as it just undermined my confidence and motivation. It was much better to focus on myself and the small improvements I could make to my own form each week. That way I always saw progress.

2. Participate fully, but exercise autonomy in how you participate.

There were many exercises that were far beyond my current level of flexibility. But, brilliantly, Lina gave multiple choices for each move so that everyone could get involved at whichever stage they were at. If you couldn't stretch your knee fully in this way, why not try this variation instead?

3. Mastery is a gradual journey, not a destination.

Over the course of a session, I found myself being able to do a little more of each exercise. But I didn't try to become a true yogi overnight. Again, such high expectations will only drain you of your desire to keep going.

4. Experience flow in all its wonder.

As you engage, you'll find yourself getting lost in the activity and perhaps losing your sense of time. The first five minutes of the session were excruciating; the last five minutes whizzed by. If you can experience that flow, you're already halfway there.

5. Pre-commit to your new habit.

If you enjoy your foray into something new, make some immediate pre-commitments – to yourself and others. I've already booked my next sessions with Lina for this and next week.

6. Transfer your confidence.

We now know that the chemical myelin is critical for lifelong learning. Your foray into a new skill is a natural way to build new layers of it in your body. In learning something new, we are building momentum in our bodies to learn other new things. Use it!

I may never be the most agile and beautiful yogi to watch. But I discovered something that I (unexpectedly) deeply enjoyed.

Lifelong learning isn't just an obligation. It's part of the beauty of what life has to offer. Embrace it. If I can be an aspiring yogi, you really can aspire to be anything you want.

46: Walk the Tightrope: Committing to Career Change

A career change, especially at midlife, can be a scary prospect. But it can also be the most fulfilling and valuable step we can take – a new leap in our lifelong learning journey.

I now think of career change as like walking a tightrope between our established selves and our new desired selves. For a time, you will have to keep your balance and hold your nerve, walking through a no-man's land of uncertainty about whether you can make the leap into unknown territory.

It's been three years since I embarked full-time on my own career change journey, supporting leaders experiencing inflection moments.

Here are four principles that I've learned that will help us stay on that tightrope and remain open to possibilities:

1. Know your authentic motivation.

I wanted to work across sectors in my new career. Many people told me it would be easier and faster to focus on just one. But it was the chance to support leaders across diverse organisations that motivated me. Now I work with a variety of people, from L'Oréal and Shopify in the corporate world to the Chandler Institute of Governance to leading non-profits such as Teach For All. Looking back, I'm glad I stayed true to my inner voice.

2. Be open to new connections and crossovers in your career.

I started my journey helping leaders build motivating cultures in their organisations, building on themes in my book Intrinsic. But I found that, through this work, I also got drawn into helping those same remarkable leaders negotiate new directions for themselves and their organisations and unleash the potential of their teams. In other words, I was helping the leaders I worked with to navigate their key inflection moments – and that's become my career focus. But I learned all this by discovery, not by design.

3. Seek out different types of nurturers to help you evolve.

I'm hugely grateful to three groups of nurturers on my journey. The first group helped me discover new forms of insight and knowledge. The second wanted to be pioneer partners with me in this important new work. The third group generously helped me connect with leaders in new sectors. All three groups were invaluable in helping me to evolve in a new direction.

4.Take small 'rites of passage' steps in your development of new mastery.

I took small steps towards my career transition over time. For example, my foray into the corporate world started with me giving short keynotes at Amazon and Mercedes-Benz AG. That developed into intensive one-off workshops, and now I carry out fully fledged year-long programmes of work. Take small steps and they will soon become miles.

At this point, I'm feeling a lot more established in my new career direction, and my company, Intrinsic Labs, has evolved accordingly!

Career change is rarely easy, and it can feel like we are always about to fall off the tightrope. So I hope these guiding principles can help us to swallow our fear and stay on it.

47: Jumping off the Treadmill: How to Keep Your Learning Perspective Fresh

Do you want to enjoy a truly perspective-changing break from work? A break that really alters your outlook on life and your career?

As leaders, we end up running so fast on the treadmill that we barely have a moment to breathe and reflect on what our real direction should be; whether that's to take a career risk, lead our teams differently or be a different (and hopefully better) partner or parent.

The breaks we take from work – especially in the summer or during the Christmas season in Western countries, when everyone follows a similar rhythm – help us to create that reflective space to pause. And to see ourselves, our colleagues and our loved ones in a different light.

Here are six tips I have found useful to regain a fresh perspective when we take a breather from work:

1. Read and listen, but to something different.

If you normally binge on business books, now is the time to pick up those novels by the bedside drawer. If you're a podcast hound, check out the latest Afrobeats or classical music. What a great time to explore more of what life has to offer. Different influences like this, even if they aren't related to our work, can alter our thoughts and experiences, opening up new worlds for us.

2. Limit daily contact that might trigger your work brain so as to give your mind time to wander.

Switch on your out of office and ask colleagues to call (not text or message) if there's something really urgent. You'll find that few things really are. But if something does blow up, you can still respond.

3. Set up different rhythms and routines.

If you're a lark (early bird), now's the time to play owl. If you like to be indoors, get out and boost that vitamin D. If you get mildly seasick (as I do), get on that boat with your son. Changing your routine challenges you, which encourages you to think and act in new ways. It boosts your well-being and creativity, and it helps you experience different possibilities.

4. Be fully 'in the moment' for your loved ones and friends.

Often, we give the remnants – the leftovers – of our time to our loved ones. Now is our chance to reverse that trend. Take a deep breath and relax a few hours before you get on that plane/train/car, so you enter a different space. By giving your loved ones all of you, you'll have all of them in return, and you'll see different sides of each other.

When you come back from your break, reflect on what new things you've learned and how you've evolved. You'll be surprised at how doing a few simple things can impact you in a short amount of time. You'll also likely be refreshed and better prepared for the next leg of your career journey.

48: Should I Stay or Should I Go? Deciding When to Leave a Role

Every leader has to decide when it's time to move on from their position. I struggled with this question myself as a leader and founder.

The important thing is to stop and reflect before you take that leap. Here are four questions I suggest every leader ask themselves in this situation:

1. Are you still motivated to solve wicked problems, or have you become the motivational problem?

Leaders often step into their roles to solve wicked problems – problems with no easy technical solution. Brexit was a great example of this – an issue so complex and intractable that it became the prime issue of debate in UK politics for years. But there is only so much fuel in our motivational tanks. Often, we end up running on empty as new wicked problems – from the war in Ukraine to the cost-of-living crisis – emerge. If you have nothing left as a leader to tackle these big issues, it's time to move on.

2. Are your team members still motivated by achieving their purpose, or are they motivated purely by your preservation and their own?

Purpose is about helping and serving others. But it's easy as a leader to subvert the motivations of our teams towards self-preservation. Boardrooms and cabinets can then quickly become medieval courts, with narcissism and entitlement deeply setting in. If we then 'sacrifice' these very colleagues on the self- preservation altar (by forcing them to defend our own lying, for example), there's almost no turning back.

3. Can you attract a team that is better than you?

It's easy to believe that 'only I can do it'. But the litmus test of a great leader is the ability to forge a leadership team that is individually and collectively better than you are. If you've got to this fortunate position, you can focus your time on nurturing your team – helping them to become the best version of themselves and reach places they wouldn't have gotten to otherwise. But if you're struggling to fill key positions with warm bodies, it's a sign that the game is up. Your presence there is to the detriment of the team and its future.

4. Are you going to leave your organisation in a better or worse place than you found it?

Leaders are ultimately stewards and custodians of their organisations. They should be building and improving the organisational fabric each day, so their successor inherits a stronger legacy. But if we undermine and weaken that very fabric, particularly when it comes to the integrity of our office, it's fatal.

The stay-or-go question is a deeply personal one, and also deeply contextual. I hope that answering these questions honestly will help you make the right call for yourself – and for those you lead.

If this is an area of interest for you, I share more ideas on how to find motivation as a leader in my book Intrinsic, including ways to improve leadership and motivation in politics.

I hope this is a useful framework for leaders everywhere who are struggling to know if it's time to move on.

49: Calming the Fire: Emotional Intelligence and Learning to Forgive

Last year I returned from South Africa where I'd been supporting Llewellyn Fredericks, Adliya van Niekerk CA(SA), Allan van der Meulen and Marlon Parker. Four remarkable leaders who are reimagining early childhood care and workforce readiness across this fascinating country.

On my last day I made a trip to Robben Island.

I had no idea I would be shown round by an actual former prisoner, Tom Moses. I couldn't quite believe that someone who had suffered so much injustice could still have the strength to tell his story.

As leaders, we will almost inevitably suffer injustice in how we're treated. It may be unfair criticism – or even an attack – from a board member, an investor, a client or a colleague. And these can hurt. As leaders, we are the closest to the firing line. We can feel exposed, even naked.

Tom's story reminded me that we can often (unwittingly) do the same to others. In our rush to move fast and decisively, we can trample on people's feelings. We can shatter their confidence or sense of emotional safety. And these scars – this collateral damage – can take a long time to heal.

In my own career, there have been times where I've felt unfairly treated – including in one situation where I never felt 'enough'. My boss couldn't see me as a unique person, always comparing my behaviour to his own. In the end, I left that job, but the emotional fallout took me a long time to recover from.

When I look back, the memories are still painful, but I have more compassion for the person concerned. I also feel a sadness that he wasn't able to see the potential in others that differed from his own and what a missed opportunity that was. On my end, the experience made me think, Screw it!, encouraging me to make the jump into the non-profit sector – something I may not have had the courage to do in 'normal times'.

Even if you can't fully forgive the person that hurts you, you can at least have empathy for the conditions that made them behave in that way. Empathy is not a magic bullet, but it can help us to put things in perspective – and encourage us to be kinder to others and to ourselves.

So, here's a suggestion: whenever we're the victim of unfair criticism, let's trust the positive intent of the person.

And when it comes to our own leadership, remember that there is a real person behind the target or deliverable. If we need to give tough feedback, let's remind the person why we're doing it – often it's out of concern for them and the organisation.

And most of all, if we get something wrong, let's apologise and own it. If we learn – like Tom – to forgive, there's a better path ahead for us.

50: Twists and Turns: Trusting the Value of the Crooked Learning Journey

Learning to learn.

I think it's the most important muscle we need to exercise in our lives – and across the world – today.

Last year, I attended the Kellogg College Annual Writers Reading, on its Masters in Creative Writing programme. The acclaimed Jason Allen-Paisant emblazoned the evening with his poetry and prose, but all 20 writers who shared their work brought remarkable brightness.

I was a proud member of the programme's inaugural cohort, way back in 2005. (Yes, I do feel decidedly ancient when I write that.)

At the time, there was a fierce debate about whether you could 'teach' creative writing in the first place. Whether it would snuff out all creativity and lead to conformity.

And (surprise, surprise) whether a hallowed place like Oxford should even delve into such areas.

Course founder Clare Morgan and her co-originators deserve a Nobel prize in determination for getting the course approved.

The quality of what I listened to felt like a resounding repudiation of any such concerns. Why was it such a magical programme for me?

I had always loved writing. The programme made me feel like a true writer. Through it I met other writers, and that gave me a sense of identity. It made me treat this craft seriously. It forced me to exercise an important muscle that had always been part of my soul and body.

At the event, I felt something of a black sheep. My first book was published almost 15 years after I graduated, and it was in non-fiction rather than as a novelist or a poet. (But who knows for the future? It's never too late.)

I now teach at Oxford, but at Saïd Business School rather than in creative writing.

But I hope my writing on leadership is sharper and more powerful as a result of the journey. And that my teaching is somewhat richer with images and metaphor.

What I have learned from my journey is to trust the learning-to-learn goddess. (Yes, she's a goddess this time, rather than a seductress or temptress.)

Here are some principles that this learning-to-learn goddess has taught me:

- Learning is so important at inflection moments. As we've explored, there are rarely any 'right answers' at these junctures. We need (as we've seen) to launch into inflection moments with a sharp and unique perspective and direction. And although we need to believe in this perspective and direction, we must also remember to be open to learning and refining that perspective over time.

- Often, however, we do the exact opposite as leaders. We believe we've gained all the knowledge we need because that's how we got here. We tend to cordon ourselves off among people who share the same background and interests (remember our discussion around networks). But that stifles us as it creates an echo chamber.

- Instead of being scared of the new, we need to think of learning as the key to achieving the pillars of authenticity, connection and excellence that we've explored. Because learning provides the reflective space for us to integrate these elements deeply into our careers and lives.

- As leaders, we can and must to do things differently. First, we can intentionally set up our lives so we are exposed to new sources of learning – whether that's listening to different voices or being open to new experiences. Second, we need to be open to serendipity – that insight your colleague provides that at first feels shocking and inconvenient but which you soon know you should incorporate in how you navigate this inflection moment. Most importantly, we then need to create the space to build these areas of learning into our daily leadership behaviours – and this also takes intentionality.

The Learning Goddess is rarely linear. She doesn't often lead us to what we initially expect. But she also needs us to sit up and listen and be intentional at the right times.

But the twists and turns of the journey she takes us on – showing us our ability to take ideas and practices from different realms – is priceless. It leads to new paths and possibilities we would never have envisaged beforehand.

And, most of all, however we harness it, the muscle memory never fades. I will always be a writer.

Because, across whatever I do, I will always love the process of writing.

51: Celebrate the Leap: Valuing Action over Inaction at Inflection Moments

Every couple of days, a parcel of some sort arrives at our house. But over 2022, three such arrivals felt particularly special:

1. The Mandarin translation of my book Intrinsic, from my agent Rachel Mills and my Taiwanese publisher.

2. A box of perfumes from my first major corporate client, L'Oréal (so I smell even nicer too!)

3. A box of Scottish goodies from Imaginable Futures, where I provided leadership development support to their portfolio companies (another personal first).

They were all lovely gestures in themselves. But they meant so much more because they symbolised new inflection moments for me in my own career change journey.

In our society, people are often recognised based on tenure (five years at a job, say) or on performance. We see their value in them being established in what they do – in their success over the long term.

But we rarely celebrate people when they make a big change in their careers. We don't always recognise personal inflection moments.

But why? These are the points at which someone has stretched themselves to the limit. Where they have taken a true risk. And where they may be feeling a sharp sense of imposter syndrome (as I certainly did at each of these inflection points) as they begin again at the bottom of the metaphorical ladder. Isn't this leap of bravery worth celebrating?

When I spoke to Milly Richardson – chief people officer at Vitesse – she told me about feeling that sense of being able to step into something bigger than you at an inflection moment. It's a point at which you just have to suspend judgment, jump and take the plunge. It may feel surreal and destabilising.

Recognising people at these inflection moments therefore makes a career leap feel concrete and valid: like a caterpillar transforming into a butterfly rather than a lemming taking a leap off the edge of a cliff. Supporting this level of ambition is powerful.

The biggest risk in our careers and lives today is that we are weighed down by how we perceive the cost of action. The fear, the risk of making that jump, can feel overwhelming, particularly if we are successful at what we already do.

What we often forget to recognise is that the cost of inaction is so much heavier. It can weigh on our minds and haunt us for years.

This is a principle that applies to us as leaders, but also to those we lead. At inflection moments, the cost of inaction is so much greater than the cost of action. So, let's recognise and celebrate ourselves and others when we have the courage to act.

Here's hoping that we can be celebrated as leaders for our courage to take a leap into the unknown. And if you want to recognise someone important to you, what better moment than when they have acted at an inflection moment?

52: Vanquishing Impostor Syndrome: Learning How to Leap into Leadership

Imposter syndrome can be a tricky adversary when we are about to make a career change.

What's the best way to deal with it when we need to step up into a leadership position? When we need to inspire confidence in others?

This year we celebrated an incredible moment of freedom for Nazanin Zaghari-Ratcliffe when she was released from Iran after six years of imprisonment.

My wife, Aida, recently met Nazanin's husband, Richard, who's an accountant by training. He had no experience in communications or campaigning, yet he masterminded an incredible campaign to keep his wife's plight in the public eye. Because he had to.

Some of our greatest leaders – from Gandhi to Dr King – were not 'groomed' for leadership. They leapt into leadership because they had to.

So many leaders I meet want to arrive in their roles fully baked, but that's just not realistic. Indeed, the people around us often want us to arrive half-baked so they can be part of the journey.

We should remember that when we feel like we don't have the required background or experience to succeed in a new leadership role.

Here are four key lessons for those of us thinking about stepping up to become leaders who are feeling scared:

1. Don't let perfection be the enemy of the good.

We are all far from perfect. But if you don't step up to the plate, remember that no one else likely will. Take the step, but be kind to yourself. Don't expect immediate success, and allow yourself to fail as you learn. And share your vulnerability with others that you want to bring on the journey. Don't hide it like a guilty secret. Everyone is likely feeling the same.

2. Surround yourself with great nurturers.

They will be our eyes and ears and help round out our sharper edges. The best ones won't try to give you answers but will know what questions to ask at the right time. They help us see new patterns and connections. They help us get to places we wouldn't have gotten to otherwise. And they help us learn in the best way possible – by drawing out our own insight.

3. Show humility and openness.

Admit when you don't know the answer, and be open to others' ideas and curious about new perspectives. Showing humility is not a weakness; it will draw people to you. It shows that you put the mission and others above your own interests. If we hide our true selves and play games because of our fears, we'll encourage others to do the same.

4. Dissolve yourself into your purpose, so you don't have time to be self-conscious.

In life and death situations like Nazanin's, there simply isn't time for self-consciousness. But in everyday leadership situations, too, try to lose yourself in the problem you are solving. Purpose – the sense of helping and serving others – is the most powerful motivator and helps us focus inwards rather than worrying about what other people think.

No one wants to be in a situation like Richard's. But we can all learn a lot from how he stepped up and truly led in an extraordinary situation, when it really mattered.

53: The Beauty of Sunsets: Having the Courage to Reinvent Ourselves

You've heard of fear of failure. But what about fear of reinvention?

In my first book, Intrinsic, I wrote about the spiralling rates of anxiety among our young people and the role of social media and comparison culture in fuelling a 'fear of failure' youth epidemic.

For the established leaders that I work with, however, fear of failure is far less relevant. Most have successfully climbed the ladder; they are already seriously accomplished. But this brings with it a new fear. As a result of scaling these heights, their identity and sense of self-worth can become deeply embedded in the 'what' of their success.

Then an inflection moment arises. And with it the opportunity to navigate their organisations and themselves towards a fundamentally better and more exciting place.

The challenge is that with the possibility of a new sunrise, we often need to accept a sunset over what has created our existing success. With a new direction, our original approach, style and methods may become obsolete, even if they were what made us stand out previously. This might feel scary, both emotionally as well as rationally, and destabilising.

Thinkers like the late Clayton Magleby Christensen have written about the 'innovator's dilemma' – how those inventing new products are held back by the fear of how they will ultimately undermine their existing products. And we know the cautionary tales of Blockbuster and Kodak, which resisted the opportunity to reimagine and reinvent themselves because they had such profitable legacy businesses.

But sunsets can also be beautiful.

The challenge is to look at reinvention using the right lens. We may be tempted to see it through the prism of the status quo – our success in that moment. Instead, we need to compare it to what would happen if the status quo were allowed to continue. In this context, almost always, our current good fortune is unsustainable.

And we also forget the real root causes of our existing success. It's often not the 'what' of our methods and tools. Instead, our success often reflects 'how' we have gone about things – our drive, our curiosity and our focus on the people we are helping to serve. The more human qualities that almost always lead to success. Hopefully, that realisation allows us to be open to change – and to let go of the 'what'.

The reality is that inflection moments are composed of both sunrises and sunsets.

And if we refuse to fully reinvent ourselves, to embrace the sunset, we will never open ourselves up to the brilliant radiance of a brand new sun.

Reflective Questions from Section 5: Learning to Learn

1. *What has been the role of lifelong learning in your career and life to date? How can you accelerate it going forward?*

2. *How can you keep your perspective fresh and open?*

3. *How can you apply the principles of learning new things to a couple of areas that you want to focus on?*

4. *Who do you want to prioritise learning and co-creating with?*

5. *How can you offset any risks of impostor syndrome as you go on your lifelong learning journey?*

6. *What areas of your work identity call for a reinvention? How will you best achieve that?*

DIAL FRAMEWORK RECAP:

Dare a new direction (the hour hand)

Ignite potential in ourselves and others (the minute hand)

Align motivations (the second hand)

Learn to learn (the watch dial)

Final Thoughts

I hope that, through reading this book, you've embraced the fact that not all leadership time is created equal.

And I hope that you embrace your inflection moment for what it is: an opportunity.

A chance to articulate your unique perspective on a problem that really matters to you, and to see it turn into an authentic and unique direction that gives you and others focus.

To nurture potential in yourself and in those that you lead, and to create cultures that nurture the potential of all.

To align the motivations of others and feel deep purpose and connection in yourself – and know how to seize it.

To truly adopt the orientation and 'muscles' of a lifelong learner.

I hope you'll harness your inflection moments to achieve what I consider to be the core definition of leadership: to empower and enable others to reach places they wouldn't have reached otherwise.

To move from tired, cynical and despondent to feeling deeply alive and driven by the possibilities of an unpredictable and fast-changing world.

To be truly leading.

To be the leaders we and others truly deserve us to be. To be the custodians of a better world.

All these are tough asks in our day-to-day world, but inflection moments enable us to reach for what can feel like the impossible – and make it possible. Whether it's an inflection moment at a personal, organisational or societal level (or, often, all three at once).

Inflection moments require a lot from us – most of all, elasticity: the ability to step into the new, while still harnessing the best of the old.

They're not easy to navigate, but if we do so with an open mind, we'll futureproof our own lives and the lives of so many others.

That's the opportunity right in front of us if we seize the fierce urgency of now.

Acknowledgements

Inflection couldn't have happened without the support of the hundreds of Leaders I've worked over these past years, across so many diverse sectors and countries. I've learned so much from all you and I hope I have done some justice to the insights I have gained from our collaboration. Thank you.

I'm also incredibly grateful to my LinkedIn Community who provided generous feedback, input and advice as I shared draft micro-chapters with you. Writing for a real audience made the process so much more fulfilling and real, and I hope it is a much better book for writing it this way.

I owe a huge thanks to my editor Sarah Busby for her effective yet compassionate editing of the two book drafts. Likewise to Andrew Dawson for his proofreading prowess.

Jon Cohen did a fantastic job of putting his heart and soul into the recording and production of the Inflection audio-book.

Sarah Malik, Sharitha McNeil and Dan Lovrinov were responsible for the wonderful design, all the way through to getting it to print.

Hannah Cary and Angelika Szpregiel drove the outreach to press and helped me get the word out.

As always, I'm grateful to my wife Aida, and my two young boys Eashan and Sayan, for their patience. Being a writer can take its toll on being a husband and a dad, and I'm often imperfect at all three roles. Thank you for being and bearing with me.

I'm lucky to have supportive parents, and a wide-circle of friends, who have offered encouragement all the way through my journey.

Inflection is so much richer for having your collective support and help.

About the Author: Sharath Jeevan OBE

Sharath is a globally recognised authority on leadership at inflection moments. As an acclaimed advisor, facilitator and author, he supports a diverse range of leaders and organisations to safely navigate their own inflection moments and futureproof their success using an innovative guided journey process.

These include pre-eminent global corporations, public sector organisations, non-profits, growth businesses and venture funds. Sharath also teaches leadership at both University of Oxford and Cambridge University.

Sharath's groundbreaking first book, Intrinsic, received widespread acclaim, including from former prime ministers and fellow authors Dan Heath and Nir Eyal.

Sharath was awarded an OBE in the Queen's 2022 New Year's Honours and an honorary doctorate for his contributions to the field.

He holds degrees from Cambridge University, University of Oxford and INSEAD and has worked at Strategy& and eBay. He founded and led two education organisations – STiR Education and Teaching Leaders – which collectively impacted more than 10 million children across 40,000 schools in the UK, US, India, East Africa, Indonesia and Brazil.

Sharath's work has been featured in a wide range of global media, including The Economist, The New York Times, CNN, Forbes, Inc, CNBC, Financial Times and The Telegraph. Sharath writes regularly on LinkedIn for a wide audience.

Sharath lives in London with his wife and two boys.

Printed in Great Britain
by Amazon

38223530R00069